LOOKING AROUND

Mississippi

WITH WALT GRAYSON

LOOKING AROUND
Mississippi
WITH WALT GRAYSON

THE ELECTRIC POWER ASSOCIATIONS OF MISSISSIPPI is pleased to present this limited edition of *Looking Around Mississippi with Walt Grayson* by Walt Grayson.

These stories and photographs reflect a personal view of Mississippi's natural beauty, culture, and history through the eyes of a writer enamored of his native state.

The Electric Power Associations of Mississippi is the Ridgeland-based service organization for twenty-five distribution electric power associations and one generation-and-transmission electric power association in the state. We are proud to have served these locally owned electric cooperatives for more than sixty years.

This book reflects our pride in being an integral part of Mississippi's past and future. We hope it conveys how fortunate we feel to be Mississippians and to be serving Mississippians.

 **Electric Power Associations**
of Mississippi

A Touchstone Energy® Partner

A tribute to Mississippi and her people...
as many rebuild their lives after Hurricane Katrina

ELECTRIC POWER ASSOCIATIONS OF MISSISSIPPI:
Entrusted by Mississippians

ON A CHILLY, OVERCAST MORNING IN JANUARY 1934, an amazing and long-awaited event took place on Highway 9 in Pontotoc County: more than a thousand people gathered to watch a group of men lift a power pole and set it into the ground.

The mayor of Pontotoc proclaimed a holiday to mark the historic occasion. Businesses closed, and schools discharged students so they, too, could witness the spectacle. Local dignitaries and railroad officials took turns at the makeshift speaker's stand. A chorus of youngsters sang "America the Beautiful."

Why all the hoopla? That single wooden pole rising into the bleak winter sky symbolized a new era of economic progress for a region struggling, along with the rest of the country, to recover from the Great Depression. It was the first pole erected in Mississippi to bring electricity generated by the Tennessee Valley Authority (TVA) to rural residents in northeast Mississippi. As the pole rose higher, so did the hopes of all who watched. Electricity was finally coming to rural Mississippi!

At that time, less than 10 percent of rural Americans had central electric service. Mississippi's situation was even worse; less than 1 percent of its rural farms and homes had electricity. Electric service was limited mostly to towns and cities served by investor-owned utilities, which dismissed extending power lines into sparsely populated rural areas as too costly to build and maintain—and a risky investment. Who knew if farmers would even use electricity? And how could they afford it?

The means for electrifying rural Mississippi—and alleviating its poor standard of living—arrived when President Franklin D. Roosevelt created the Rural Electrification Administration (REA) in 1935. REA, now the Rural Utilities Service, offered loans to nonprofit organizations, including electric cooperatives, and other utilities for the construction of power lines, substations, and related facilities needed to take electric service deep into rural areas. Borrowers would repay the loans with interest.

Rural Mississippians jumped at the opportunity to acquire electricity. Affordable electric service would pave the way for new and badly needed improvements including electric lights, water pumps, motors, refrigeration, ovens, washing machines, and irons. Farms could modernize and become more productive. Businesses could expand markets to rural buyers eager for new electric appliances and equipment.

Farmers, mill workers, homemakers, teachers, and other rural residents united in a pioneer spirit to do for themselves what no one else would. They organized local electric power associations and knocked on doors to sign up members. They established a local board of directors, acquired REA loans, and set out to build a new breed of electric utility in America—the electric cooperative.

Mississippi was an early leader in rural electrification. Alcorn County Electric Power Association, established in 1934 in Corinth by TVA as an experiment, became America's first rural electric cooperative. In 1936 Monroe County Electric Power Association, in Amory, became the nation's first electric cooperative to energize its lines as an REA borrower.

COAST ELECTRIC POWER ASSOCIATION members gather to take part in the election of directors and other business affairs at their cooperative's 1948 annual meeting.

Today, twenty-five electric power associations in Mississippi distribute electricity to more than 664,000 meters in all regions of the state. Each electric power association is a locally owned cooperative governed by a board of directors that is composed of members elected by the membership.

These electric power associations deliver dependable electric service at the lowest cost possible to rural homes, suburbs, schools, churches, hospitals, businesses, manufacturers, mills, military bases, farms, and myriad other association members.

Today's electric utility technologies would seem extraordinary to Mississippi's rural electrification pioneers. Computers facilitate nearly every step of the process, from substation operations and power line design to meter reading and accounting.

Behind all this technology is a work force that is increasingly more knowledgeable, skilled, and innovative. Electric power association decision makers—the managers and directors—are informed leaders acutely aware of the impact of their decisions on their service areas.

But as the saying goes, the more things change, the more they stay the same. Despite exponential growth and technological progress, Mississippi's electric power associations remain faithful to their founders' original vision. They built electric power associations on a foundation of service. Nothing was more important to rural electrification pioneers than the empowerment of their communities through affordable, reliable electric service.

They realized these new cooperatives could offer much more than electricity. Electric power associations quickly became integral parts of the communities they served. Through the years they have proved to be stable employers, valuable contributors to local economies, and sources of community leadership.

Local commitment is a hallmark of electric power associations; our employees, managers, and directors are local residents deeply involved in their communities. They are church leaders, youth coaches, scouting volunteers, and charitable fund-raiser organizers. They are respected citizens responsive to the needs of their service areas.

In short, our people are the source of our strength as consumer-owned electric power associations. And that will never change.

NORTHEAST MISSISSIPPI ELECTRIC POWER ASSOCIATION promoted the free installation of electric appliances with this 1957 billboard advertisement.

ELECTRIC POWER ASSOCIATIONS SPONSORED EXHIBITS at state and county fairs to teach members about electrical safety and use. Prize drawings featuring electrical appliances helped attract passersby.

Acknowledgments

I AM IN DEBT TO CHILDHOOD WINTER NIGHTS and family gatherings at my grandmother's house in Fulton, Mississippi. There was no television. We told stories for entertainment. Well, they talked. I was of the age to be seen and not heard.

After supper everybody wanted to catch up on the latest. Then someone would think of something related, and the conversation would turn in that direction for a while. Everyone had a boxcar to add on.

Hours later, silent gaps punctuated the stories as it got late, and someone would declare it was bedtime. I'd want to hear more, but usually I had already fallen asleep by then, anyway. But from such came my love for stories, hearing and telling.

What follows are boxcars of thoughts. Pods that could pretty much stand alone, or, coupled together, would form a train of conversation as they do herein. And I borrow from master storytellers I've run into on the roads of Mississippi for the contents. You'll meet many of them in the pages ahead.

NATCHEZ UNDER THE HILL was once a much larger area. The river washed most of it away. There are old photographs in the Natchez Presbyterian Church of the way it once looked.

LOOKING AROUND
Mississippi
WITH WALT GRAYSON

THE
DONNING COMPANY
PUBLISHERS

DELTA QUEEN LEAVING NATCHEZ. The old riverboat puts on a calliope concert pulling out. This is a video still from a *Look Around Mississippi* story. On my tape I have the music. Too bad books don't have sound.

MISSISSIPPI RIVER AT NATCHEZ. This is a video still frame taken from the opening of the *Look Around Mississippi* show.

BEING ON THE ROAD has its sweet surprises. We've met a ton of nice people and run across things to buy that we never knew we couldn't live without. There really are bushel loads of adventure on the roads of Mississippi.

BRIAR FARM, FULTON. This is my grandparents' house and is the hub around which my family orbits. Granddaddy built this house in 1924 and lived there until he died in 1952. That seems so long, but it's just a couple of years longer than I've lived in my house. And it seems I've been here no time at all.

KING'S TAVERN is the oldest building in Natchez. It was on the tax rolls as early as 1775.

DELTA MOONLIGHT.

STATE FAIR in Jackson sometimes comes at the same time as the October Harvest Moon. This is a video still shot of one such time.

Dear Friends,

As Governor of the State of Mississippi, I would like to thank you for your interest in my beloved home state. "Looking Around Mississippi with Walt Grayson," which features photographs of various Mississippi scenes, historic sites, and events, is a great way to discover Mississippi's unique beauty—without ever leaving the comfort of your own home.

Mississippi is known throughout the world as the "Hospitality State," and for good reason. After Hurricane Katrina—the worst natural disaster in American history—stories of ordinary people displaying extraordinary courage and uncommon selflessness have been extremely common. From the very beginning Mississippians have been helping themselves, and God bless them, helping their neighbors. The unselfish, even selfless attitude of people who've lost everything is awe-inspiring to me. Their will makes me strong in my determination to make sure we help these great people recover and rebuild and renew South Mississippi and the Coast to heights that are equal to that hospitable spirit.

It is our shared memories and regard for tradition that give Mississippians a strong sense of community. We know things that really matter endure — traditions like respect for the land, for each other and for a job well done. Keeping a firm grip on where we came from, Mississippians reach out to meet the future halfway.

Mississippi's music and literary traditions have gained the state worldwide fame. The world's largest collection of blues music is housed at the University of Mississippi Blues Archives. Elvis Presley, called by some the greatest single influence on popular culture in the 20th century, was born and raised in Mississippi.

I hold a special place in my heart for my hometown of Yazoo City. Known as the "Gateway to the Delta," Yazoo City sits atop lush rolling hills rising from the fertile flatlands of the Mississippi Delta. I grew up in these kudzu-covered hills and cherish many fond memories of my picturesque small town.

Whether you're listening to the Delta blues or simply enjoying a glass of tea with a neighbor, Mississippi is the place that captures the Southern spirit of hospitality and heritage. I'll always have a special place in my heart for this state--it truly is a wonderful place to call home.

Sincerely,

Haley Barbour
Governor

TITLE PAGE CAPTIONS

Page 6:

NATCHEZ TWILIGHT. A gaslight sputters as the chorus of church bells chime, one at a time, not in competition. The ease of night settles over the city on the bluffs. Video still.

JACKSON INTHE SNOW. It is rare to see Jackson blanketed in snow. We have NEVER had a recorded snowfall on Christmas Day in Jackson. So we snap pictures like this in February or March and put them on the front of next year's Christmas cards and pretend.

NATCHEZ NOON. I just liked the shot. This is a video still shot from a *Look Around Mississippi* story.

Page 7:

THIS WINDOW at the old Sisters of Mercy Convent wouldn't stay closed for the longest time after the City of Vicksburg took over the complex. It nearly started a ghost story. But we all know there's no such thing as ghosts.

The Donning Company Publishers
184 Business Park Drive, Suite 206
Virginia Beach, Virginia 23462–6533

Steve Mull, General Manager
Barbara Buchanan, Office Manager
Kathleen Sheridan, Senior Editor
Amanda D. Guilmain, Graphic Designer
Amy Thomann, Imaging Artist
Mary Ellen Wheeler, Proofreader
Scott Rule, Director of Marketing
Stephanie Linneman, Marketing Coordinator
Cindy Smith, Project Research Coordinator

Neil Hendricks, Project Director

Library of Congress Cataloging-in-Publication Data

Grayson, Walt, 1949-
  Looking around Mississippi with Walt Grayson / by Walt Grayson.
     p. cm.
  Includes index.
  ISBN 1-57864-333-3 (alk. paper)
  1. Mississippi--Social life and customs--Anecdotes. 2. Mississippi--History, Local--Anecdotes. I. Title.
  F341.6.G73 2005
  976.2--dc22

                    2005025364

Printed in the United States of America by Walsworth Publishing Company

Foreword

IT BEGAN TO DAWN ON ME RECENTLY, AFTER TWENTY YEARS of doing feature stories at WLBT, that I'm starting to forget some of the tales I've heard and experiences I've had while out on the road shooting Look Around Mississippi stories. So I've decided to write some of them down while they are still sort of fresh on my mind.

In addition to the stories, I have hours and hours of videotape and a bunch of still photos from all over that need to be sorted and catalogued, too. And I don't want to wait so long to work on them that I forget exactly what they are of or where I shot them, and they end up being captioned like several of the shots of mountains that my sister and her husband snapped on their trip out West last summer that they waited too long to classify and had to label as "somewhere between Lincoln and Laramie."

So, before I get so far down the road that my memory sifts all of my stuff to simply "somewhere between Batesville and Biloxi," I thought I'd give it a whack and try to stack the photos into related piles.

And maybe it wouldn't be a bad idea to start telling the story of all of this back before the beginning; before all I did for a living was run around the state with a camera and a microphone looking for oddities and out-of-the-way places. Start telling this story back about the time I realized I wanted to do things like take pictures, maybe not as a living but as a serious hobby at least. Starting there may help explain why I chose some of the kinds of stories that I shot later, and why I snapped some of the pictures that ended up in this book.

There is one particular photograph I remember seeing back in my teenage years that struck me as being particularly good. This photography scrutiny was taking place almost accidentally while I was doing something else. I was working my first job in broadcasting while I was a junior in high school in Greenville, Mississippi.

It was an excellent photograph to start with. Brooding darks offset by highlights caught in such a way as not to lose detail. The subject matter was obviously old, and it seemed to have a mixture of worlds in it. There was a dirt road reminiscent of American backwoods. And standing beside it were several huge columns suggesting that the house they once belonged to was perhaps of European influence. And there were trees growing from the tops of the columns that showed neglect. But not the kind of neglect that had led to disaster but had molded the whole thing into a work of art.

The photograph was in the office of radio station WJPR, where I worked the sign-on shift, then went to school and returned for a couple of hours in the afternoon. The picture was my escape from reality.

Stretching my legs during network newscasts, I'd walk up front and look out the glass door at the traffic passing on Broadway, imagining all those car radios were tuned to me. And then I'd pause in front of the photograph on my way back to the control room. I saw it as a whole. And then I'd study details of it. I'd follow the dirt road beside the columns until it was obscured by the tangled mass of vines spilling from the floor of the adjacent woods, flowing as if liquid toward the ruin itself.

And because it was a photograph, meaning this was a picture of something actually real somewhere in the world, I wondered where it was. I'd decided it must be the remains of some old castle in Europe somewhere.

Then one day the station manager walked up while I was woolgathering in front of the photograph, and I asked him where this was. I was flabbergasted when he told me it was in Mississippi—the ruins of the Windsor plantation house, no more than 120 miles away from where we were standing right then, down in Claiborne County at Port Gibson.

FOSTER MOUND CHURCH WINDOW. Many colors don't mean you've found the end of the rainbow. While looking for the oldest tombstone death date, I stumbled upon this church window. I never found the grave.

DUNLEITH, NATCHEZ, is another of the city's antebellum homes. Dunleith, like many others, is a B&B. Nice place to stay to see what the Old South was like.

MARTHA'S STORE, VICKSBURG, attracts its share of the curious. Martha's husband, Rev. Dennis, said he would build her a palace if she would marry him. She did. Here it is.

I had never heard of it and had never heard of Port Gibson at that time that I can recall. All of this was a new Mississippi to me. It was somewhere apart from my familiar levees and Indian mounds and eternal cotton fields and sloughs and bayous of my Delta childhood.

But the sudden awareness that Mississippi had something like the ruins of that beautiful house at Windsor turned on a light in me that allowed me to think of Mississippi in other terms than how the state had been portrayed on the nightly newscasts of the major TV networks of the '60s. Unconsciously, it started me on a journey of discovery and amazement that has lasted until this very moment. And will, no doubt, go on as long as I do.

So that said, here we go *Looking Around Mississippi*. We'll hit it with the zeal of youth, since the roots of everything I've done run back to my youth. And we'll sit and catch our breath when our youthful spirit outruns the body that has unmercifully insisted on aging every year since it was a youth.

Ready to go? Good!

Then let's rest a minute and we'll get started.

Contents

HOUSE AT QUITO. The old sharecroppers' cabin is just across the road from one of Robert Johnson's graves at a place named Quito. Shortened from mosquito. Really.

To my wife Jo
WHO TRAVELED EVERY MILE OF THIS
BOOK WITH ME.

THE PIANO-SHAPED HEADSTONE is just behind the Confederate graves in Vicksburg Cemetery. Like the Pharaohs, we try to take into death the things we loved in life.

Windsor & River

COUNTRY

MAYBE IT WAS ABOUT 1985. I don't think it was any later than that when I first saw Windsor in person.

It was one of those days after which things weren't as they had been before, but I didn't realize it right away. An epiphany? Maybe. But it was a slow-motion one before it all played itself out.

I had already served a seventeen-year hitch in radio and had graduated to television via an introductory career as a weekend weather anchor while still working full-time at WSLI radio in Jackson.

All that weekend weathering led to a full-time weather job with the added duty of reporting "occasional" stories at WLBT in 1984. I thought occasional might mean a couple of stories a week.

Ended up, news director Bert Case really had in mind for me to do a story in the afternoon to air in the 6:00 p.m. news and then another one after supper to air at ten before I ever got the chance to put my 10:00 p.m. weathercast together.

I guess it was about a year after I started working at WLBT that photographer Chuck Rook and I had been assigned to Port Gibson to do one of those "occasional" stories.

Now, I hadn't thought about the ruins of Windsor all that much since those days back in the lobby of WJPR in Greenville when I'd look at the old black-and-white photograph. But after Chuck and I finished shooting all the needed material for our story, we had a little free time left, and I had spotted the sign pointing the way to Windsor. On a whim I asked Chuck if it would be okay if we went out to see it. (The photographers drove.) Sure.

WINDSOR FOOTBALL. Nice catch.

Had we not gone to Windsor that day, I might be doing something entirely different for a living right now.

Following the ridge top where possible, the road twists and turns a great deal and ducks from shadow to light and back as it weaves and bobs the seven miles from Port Gibson to Windsor.

It seemed as though it took a long time to get there. But then, rounding a bend, there it was—the columns of Windsor rising up from the plowed fields around it as if it had been planted and grown there like ancient tree trunks. That was back before Windsor was surrounded by the pine plantation that hides it today. Back then, you could still see it from the main road as you approached it. It was a pivotal moment for this modern-day descendant of the Old South, seeing Windsor rising up from the earth, sort of like Scarlett making her way back to Tara, where she vows never to be hungry again.

WINDSOR IN WINTER. The ruins of Windsor stand fully exposed under the leafless pecan trees that surround it in winter. My first introduction to Windsor was through an old black-and-white photograph.

We pulled up on the far side of the circle drive and stopped. It was a hazy day. Not really cloudy, but no sharp shadows either. A perfect day for shooting video with the old tube-type cameras that WLBT used out in the field back then.

I got Chuck to shoot some footage of the columns and the road leading up to them and the old caretaker's cabin that used to stand out to the side of the ruins. And we got shots of the breeze blowing through the Johnson grass in the field out in front of Windsor, with the columns out of focus in the background.

The story we had been assigned to do went on the newscast as scheduled that night. But I held onto the Windsor footage and wrote some narration to go with it, and in just a few days we got a chance to air the feature. After that, I sort of began a shift away from hard news to exploring the history, culture, and beauty of Mississippi.

So at seventeen I first saw the photograph at the radio station. Then, seventeen years later, another whole lifetime away from when I had first discovered it in the picture, I saw Windsor in person. And now, about that many more years later, I am finally doing features exclusively.

I guess I didn't want to reach my peak too early.

Eudora Welty called this part of Mississippi "River Country." Generally, it encompasses that area bounded by Grand Gulf (the extinct town, not the power plant) to the north down to Rodney (another extinct town) to the south. The Windsor ruins are the heart of it.

I understand Ms. Welty wasn't aware of Windsor until she just ran up on it while working as a photographer with the WPA during the depression. That would be something like just running up on the Pyramids, unaware they existed.

I was not all that familiar with Eudora Welty's work the time I first saw Windsor for myself. And her collection of photographs of such places as Windsor and Church Hill and Rodney were still years away from being pub-

ROAD TO WINDSOR. The seven or so miles from Port Gibson to Windsor rises over bluff tops and dives into bayou bottoms. And each season brings another show of nature, as with this spring dogwood.

STANDING ROOM ONLY. The vertical lines of the stately columns of Windsor are a mere shadow of the grandeur of the home when it was still standing and in use.

GRAND GULF REBURIAL. Two black Union soldiers whose graves were in danger of falling into a gully were moved and reburied by a contingent of Confederate Civil War reenactors. Still video frame from *Look Around* story.

GRAND GULF RIFLE PITS. The earthworks were dug by Confederate defenders on the bluff top at Grand Gulf and have been left pretty much untouched since then. Grant's march video still frame.

GRAND GULF SOLDIER. There are several black Union soldiers buried in Grand Gulf Cemetery. Here is the grave of Mose Williams of the 64th U.S. Colored Infantry.

RIVER COUNTRY ROAD. These magic roads travel not only distances but back in time, also. This is a video still from a *Look Around* story about River Country.

lished. As a matter of fact, I was discovering those places for myself at about the same time I started discovering her writings and pictures of them from sixty years earlier.

It was a kick to read she had many of the same feelings about exploring River Country that I had. I just wish I had written it first.

After I purchased my own television camera, the *Look Around Mississippi* series became official. My first *Look Around Mississippi* story was about the ruins of Windsor. It was my tribute to the place for awakening me from my teenage stupor all those years ago when I found out there was more to the world than just what I saw on the way to work and back home.

Windsor strikes different people in different ways. I can't think of a single time I have ever been there that other people didn't drive up to see it. The usual response is a sense of awe at the size of the place as you instinctively try to imagine how large the house must have been before it burned.

One fellow from up North somewhere who drove up with his wife must have been having a bad day. He was fussing about Port Gibson, griping he had heard it was "too beautiful to burn," and he hadn't seen anything beautiful about it. Then he started in on Windsor: just a bunch of bricks sticking up in the air.

Someone standing nearby apologized to him for not having more to show, but said this was all his boys from up North had left us after the Civil War. You'd have thought that would have made him hush, but it didn't. (Of course, Windsor didn't burn during the war but much later. But I thought it was a nice try.)

On the other hand, another time when we had breezed down to Windsor for an outing, a couple from Georgia had made a detour on their way home from New Orleans to come see Windsor. I asked them what they thought. The fellow said it was much like seeing the Sphinx or something.

Well, Windsor may not be among the wonders of the world, but it is one of the wonders of the South. It was finished just a year before the Civil War started. They were doing spring cleaning at the time Grant brought his troops across the

CAPITAL OF WINDSOR. Now that the Mississippi Department of Archives and History takes care of the property, very few saplings get a start in the iron capitals atop the columns at Windsor.

THE LOW ROAD. A soldier marching with Grant's army on this road commented about how the front of the column of soldiers would just vanish as the troops rounded sunken bends on the way from Bruinsburg.

BRUINSBURG SIGN. Nature is taking back all signs that civilization ever existed at Bruinsburg. The town itself is long gone.

Mississippi River at Bruinsburg. Over the railings of the porches of Windsor were hanging all sorts of quilts flapping in the breeze airing out. And the furniture had been pushed outside.

So from the river, it looked like there was a lot of activity at the house. The story goes that Grant's army thought Windsor was a fort full of soldiers with all that movement all around it. So they fired on it. And missed.

Actually, the family at Windsor was quite amiable toward Grant's troops. There was not this unified, teetotal abandonment of the United States in Southerners' loyalties when the South left the Union. Lots of folks thought it was a mistake to pull out, much like there would be misgivings if our state were to secede today.

So Grant camped his army in the cornfields at Windsor. And as a gesture for the people who lived at Windsor being so kind to him, he didn't burn the house. Oh, he burned the barns but spared Windsor.

Windsor stood for another thirty years after the War Between the States ended. Its fate was sealed at a party one Sunday night. There had been some remodeling going on at Windsor, and a guest flipped a lit cigar butt into a pile of sawdust by a window under the drapes. The smoldering butt caught the rubbish on fire, and in no time it had burned out of control and Windsor was gone, except for the columns standing there today and the wrought iron front steps that were carried to Alcorn State University and attached to the chapel building, where they still remain.

But everyone who has visited the ruins has surely tried to imagine the house as it looked before the fire. It must have been grand. Mark Twain told his steamboat passengers when they traveled past Windsor on the Mississippi River that it was a college.

Today Windsor is a ghost of time. Its shadow stands in the present, but its being is in the past, in another age. I guess I have taken more photographs and shot more videotape of Windsor than any one other single thing in the state, and I feel I have never really captured it to my satisfaction.

WINDSOR STEPS. The iron front steps of Windsor are still in use. Shortly after the house burned, they were relocated to become the main staircase to the chapel on the campus of Alcorn State University a few miles from the ruins.

WINDSOR AND THE MOON. Both are worlds apart from where we stand: the moon in miles, Windsor in time. Still video frame from a *Look Around* story.

It's hard to get on videotape something that is mostly invisible. The overwhelming component of Windsor is intangible and eludes a camera. It's something you feel rather than see—the great sense of loss. Although I never had anything approaching the grandness of Windsor personally to lose, I feel it anyway.

Maybe that's a part of it. These folks had it and lost it. The rest of us have lost it already by not ever having had it to begin with. Not that I would have wanted Windsor or any house that big. Try to heat and cool it with today's energy prices.

But we've all dreamed big things that never panned out. I remember that on my fortieth birthday my mama told me that the day she hit forty was when she realized her dreams would never come true. (Was she trying to encourage me?) I was under the impression at forty I was still a young man, and I was just beginning to dream some of my biggest dreams. I wasn't ready to set any aside.

Over the decade and a half since then, some of those dreams did come true. And some of the ones that did have since vaporized. Some are still manifesting but in ways other than I first visualized them. But much of the perfection I wanted for my life and my career is lost forever; up in smoke like Windsor, with just stubs sticking up to remind me those hopes ever existed to begin with.

The same mood that emanates from Windsor drifts across the rest of River Country and saturates places such as Grand Gulf and Rodney and Rocky Springs and Port Gibson.

Where the Big Black River empties into the Mississippi River is where the once-thriving river port town of Grand Gulf sprang up. There was a lot of water at the foot of the bluffs where the town was laid out; hence the name.

Back then, towns were built right up to the edge of the Mississippi with no regard for floods or the river's penchant for wallowing around and changing its course every so often.

Several of Grand Gulf's streets fell into the river as the Mississippi ate into the flats below the bluffs, starting the town on a decline from which it never recovered. And the river taking back some of its banks wasn't the only tragedy that struck Grand Gulf. Stroll through the town's cemetery and read the epitaphs on the tomb-

WINDSOR WHISPERS. Windsor changes mood with the time of day and with the seasons and the shifting sunlight. Here, the muted colors and flat shadows allow the old place to sit and brood.

A Native of Freedom
New York ...
...illed in th...
...Tornado at
...rand Gulf, Miss...
March 21, 185...

stones, and you can get a quick history of a yellow fever epidemic and the big torna-do that struck the town in 1853.

But the worst tragedy to hit the town was the Civil War. Grant had been training his troops on the Louisiana side of the river all winter. Then, in the spring of 1863, he started marching southward. The idea was to cross the Mississippi River south of Vicksburg somewhere and then go back northward and take Vicksburg from the land side. River assaults had been tried and had already failed.

The place Grant chose to cross over the river was Grand Gulf. But it wasn't going to be as easy as he had thought. The guns in Grand Gulf at Fort Wade, and those near the mouth of the Big Black River at Fort Cobun, were surprisingly strong against Grant's army and managed to stop the landing party from crossing the river there.

GONE WITH THE WIND. A headstone in Grand Gulf Cemetery tells some of the town's tragic history. This shot is a still frame of video from a *Look Around Mississippi* story.

CHURCH NEAR FORT COBUN. It is a rustic pile of boards that almost blends into the early-spring bare branches engulfing it. Nature is taking back much of what's been deserted in River Country.

FORT COBUN. The Confederate fort consists of earthworks set up high over where the Mississippi and Big Black Rivers flowed together. The advantage forced Grant to land farther south. Still video frame.

So Grant marched the boys a little farther south and came over at Bruinsburg. Then he promptly marched back to Grand Gulf on dry land and burned the town. Twice.

Farther south is Rodney. The first time I went there was just after we had started doing the *Look Around Mississippi* series on WLBT. I got a call from Gerrett Maris of Maris, West, and Baker Advertising in Jackson. Gerrett said his firm had adopted the old Presbyterian Church at Rodney some eight years earlier and had spent eight years of weekends repairing it and fixing it up, and they were going to have the dedication service the following Sunday. He asked me if I'd like to do a *Look Around Mississippi* story about the town and the church to air the Friday before and give them a little pre-publicity about the service. As he told me more about Rodney and the church, it sounded like a very intriguing story.

Gerrett said he had a key to the church and would draw me a map of how to get to Rodney if I'd drop by his office and pick it up. So that afternoon I did, and early the next morning I headed out to find Rodney.

I made it all the way to Lorman before I even pulled out the map. I knew Rodney was back through the bluffs out west of Lorman. So after I finished my ice cream cone from the Old Country Store, I reached into my pocket for the folded sheet of paper to see where I needed to go from there.

CANNONBALL. Filling the scar left by a Union gunboat shelling when the river ran at the foot of Rodney, a cannonball has been attached to the front wall of the Rodney Presbyterian Church.

RODNEY VOTING. I guess the people who live and do lively things like vote in Rodney would take issue with the place being referred to as a "ghost town."

RODNEY MARKER. This is a frame from a video project documenting Grant's march through River Country. The spot is Fort Wade in the front yard of the Spanish House at Grand Gulf.

WHERE THE RIVER RAN. Tractors plow soybean and cotton fields where steamboats used to plow up Mississippi River water near Rodney. The river shifted several miles west more than a hundred years ago.

OWENS CREEK WILDERNESS. In the early 1800s this waterfall was deep in the wilderness along the Natchez Trace footpath. It's still on the Trace. A convenient parking lot sits no more than twenty feet away from it today, however.

NATCHEZ TRACE SUNSET. Day is dying, but night is just coming alive. Travelers have admired the transition between the two for a long time out on the Trace.

Now, I like the South as much as anyone, but I prefer to have north at the top of my map. But as I looked at the map Gerrett had drawn, it had a big "S" at the middle top of the page. I stared blankly at the map for a minute and couldn't figure out how it was supposed to work. It seemed like any way I would try to go would only take me back toward Jackson.

Actually, it was weeks later when it dawned on me that the map was drawn as if I were in Jackson and were placing the map down in front of me toward the south. Then the lines drawn on it would take me directly to Rodney. That revelation was weeks later. That day, I didn't have a clue.

But I had come too far to turn back now. So I just headed out into the bluffs west of Lorman hoping I, like Gerrett, would just come off a hill and run into Rodney. Instead, I got—well, I started to say I got lost, but I've never been lost in Mississippi. Let's just say I was not familiar with where I was for a little while.

But the old gravel roads out in the bluffs are worth getting lost in. As they twist and wind their way through the woods, sometimes they cut through a hill and sink down in it, sort of like those old pictures of the Natchez Trace when it was just a footpath, worn deep into the ground.

In some places the bluffs on either side of the roadbed rise maybe twenty or thirty feet up over the gravel below. And on top of them, the trees grow another forty or fifty feet before they crown together way, way up overhead. I imagine there are several

MOSTLY GONE. A lone camper trailer resides on what would have been one of the busiest streets in Mississippi in the 1830s. There's less and less of Rodney every time I go back there.

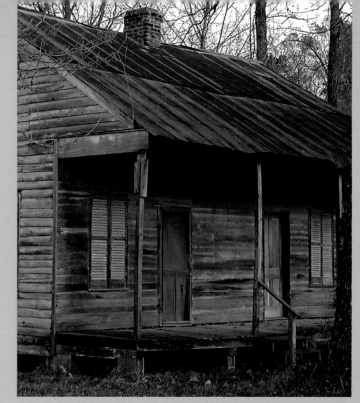

months out of the year that sunlight never reaches the surface of the road. When the leaves are still on the trees back in there, it's sort of like driving through a tunnel. So it's not the worst place in the world to be lost, er, unfamiliar with.

As a matter of fact, if you're one of those people who require a little isolation from time to time, you'd love a drive down those old gravel roads. It's a great place to go to either find yourself or lose yourself, whichever you want to do.

Finding Rodney was what I wanted to do that day, and after a few wrong turns, I came to a stretch of road that was paved and even had curbs and gutters. It descended sharply down and down and down, farther down than I realized I had been up—down into the plain where the Mississippi River had once flowed and into the heart of Rodney.

There was still enough mystery and other-worldly charm to the town back then that at first, it looked as if I had driven back in time. The price on the gas pump fixed when the store at the crossroad closed really was from another time.

Past Brumfield's store was a Creole-style cabin. Across the street from it was a huge wooden church with a silver-colored dome on top of its steeple. It had been the Rodney Baptist Church when it was built and was where an AME congregation meets now.

Turning north beside the church, I passed a wooden house that had been built up high off the ground as a protection from the frequent floods from the Mississippi River. A screened porch ran the entire length of the front of the house. An old black man lived there. He had all sorts of colorful charms and things stuck in his fence and decorating the porch and front of the house.

CREOLE CABIN, RODNEY. There are still a few old houses in the ghost town. Here's a simple bungalow that harkens back to a simpler life and a simpler time.

ZION CHURCH. Life continues even in a ghost town. What was the Rodney Baptist Church decades ago is alive and well today as the home of an AME congregation.

All those voodoo charms and things are supposed to ward off evil. They kept me away.

From that side of Rodney, the Presbyterian Church was behind me, not far from the road I had come in on, back on the side of Rodney under that first bluff that rises over the old Mississippi River bed.

COUNTRY CHURCH. There are still treasures to be found on the back roads in River Country.

COUNTRY CHURCH INTERIOR. The message and the manner are timeless. This could be today or a hundred years ago.

And then there was my goal, the Federal-style, red-brick Rodney Presbyterian Church. At that time it was in pristine shape, its green shutters in good repair and brightly painted. No grass grew in the herringbone-pattern brick sidewalks and wide steps. Inside, everything was swept and dusted.

Rodney was once a port town on the Mississippi River. It was a pretty big place prior to the Civil War. One of the historic markers in Rodney says that Zachary Taylor could well have been walking the streets there when he got news of his election as president. Mark Twain in his book *Life on the Mississippi* mentions Rodney with about as much weight as he gives Natchez and Vicksburg and Greenville.

But after the Civil War, the Mississippi River meandered west of the town a few miles and left the river port without a river. And the town dried up over time. There are still some people who live there, but Rodney is little more than a dwindling group of buildings now. The bluffs back of the town are overgrown with hardwoods, and the area is mostly populated by deer hunters.

When Gerrett first discovered Rodney, he had no idea a town was out there. He was just driving the roads through the river bluffs on a Sunday afternoon. He said he was amazed when he came down that last hill before the river bottom and saw steeples and fences and houses and things.

Since then, the Catholic church from Rodney has been moved to Grand Gulf State Park. At least one of the old homes from Rodney has been moved to Port Gibson. Many others are just gone. Houses where people used to live are empty and falling in. The voodoo house is empty—all of its colorful things have been removed, and it's pretty bland now.

RODNEY PRESBYTERIAN CHURCH. The unusual Federal-style building is a destination for the wilderness adventurer nowadays. Regular services disbanded when the town dried up.

GRAVE MARKERS, RODNEY. Palmetto fans roam at will in the Rodney Cemetery. Sometimes graves were marked by plants such as these. Unchecked, they tend to take over places.

RODNEY GRAVE. Sixty years ago, the river valley was visible beyond the edge of the bluff, and this grave's lid was slightly ajar. Everything changes.

It's as if termites invaded the town and ate large chunks of it away.

There is a grave Ms. Welty called "Rodney Cemetery with Grave Lid Ajar" in one of her photos. The grave has a boxlike concrete vault over it, and the lid covering it has been slid to one side at a corner as if someone wanted to see what was under it. The grave was at the edge of the bluff, and you could see the valley where the river ran below it at the bottom of the hill.

Well, one January day, my wife, Jo and I and Emily, our grandchild (she was about four years old then), went to the Rodney area to shoot another story about that lost part of Mississippi. We walked up the bluff behind the Presbyterian Church to get some shots of the cemetery. I had seen some of the published photographs Eudora Welty had taken of the cemetery and the town from the cemetery hill and wanted to see if there was anything still recognizable there. There wasn't much.

But I spotted the grave with the lid ajar. I felt as though I had seen a celebrity. It was there on the edge of the bluff just as in the photograph, only now, sixty-nine years later, someone had straightened the lid and put it back right. Seeing the grave like that, fixed from the way it was in the Welty photograph, my first instinct was to call out to Jo and tell her to come look and see what some vandal had done to this grave! Straightened the lid!

I met an elderly black man out in front of the Presbyterian Church several years ago. I haven't seen him since, so I don't know what happened to him. He was a tall, thin man. Wore a hat. He had on a khaki shirt and pants. He introduced himself and offered to show me Rodney. Well, I could see just about all of it from where I stood. But he began laying out the dimensions of the village. "From Mammy Judy Bayou on the north to such-and-such road on the south [only he remembered the name of the road], that's where old Judge Rodney settled."

DOWNTOWN RODNEY. The steeple of the Presbyterian Church rises above the low wood-framed remains of Rodney. The high bluff that used to reach the river rises behind the church.

RODNEY CATHOLIC CHURCH. No longer in Rodney, the church is the front piece at Grand Gulf State Park. Unlike other Rodney structures, at least the church still exists.

He went on to tell me that he often met tourists on the road in front of the old Presbyterian Church and offered to make them official members. I asked him what it was he did. "Well," he said, "I takes my hat off my head," which he demonstrated. "And I says a few words, 'Oh Lord... (on and on for a minute or so)' and when I'm through, I tells them that now they are official members. And I puts out my hat and says, 'And the first thing we're gonna do is take up a collection!'"

He got my three dollars. That was the best entertainment I'd ever had in Rodney.

Everywhere the bluffs stretched out westward enough to meet the Mississippi River, a settlement sprang up. Way down south, just north of the Louisiana state line, it was Fort Adams. Next up is Natchez. Then Rodney, Grand Gulf, and Vicksburg. Then the bluffs curve inland and the flat Delta stretches northward from Vicksburg a couple of hundred miles. And where the bluffs curve back and meet the Mississippi again lies Memphis.

When I first started exploring the bluffs, I sort of plugged into the middle of them at Windsor. But there is mystery and lore all up and down the hills and hollows of the bluffs area of the state.

OVERLOOK CHURCH. Although River Country was marked by beautiful churches and homes, rustic was also the order of the day. This restored log church is located at the Overlook west of Port Gibson.

BETHEL PRESBYTERIAN CHURCH is on the Port Gibson Battlefield. Grant's troops, heady at being undetected in enemy territory, took potshots at the steeple as they marched past in 1863.

Lower River

STORIES

MY FIRST TRIP SOUTH TO WILKINSON COUNTY came after one of the news producers at WLBT took his honeymoon driving south on Highway 61 all the way to New Orleans, stopping overnight at several places along the way. He came back to work telling me about some waterfalls at Clark Creek out west of Woodville.

He said someone had told him about this hillside with seven waterfalls on it, and he thought it might make a good *Look Around Mississippi* story. In my mind's eye I envisioned this green manicured hillside with concrete steps leading downward in a zigzag pattern with a steel handrail. And when you walked down to the bottom of the steps, you'd turn and gaze back up at seven waterfalls cascading down the hill behind you.

Nice thought. I should be writing fiction with an imagination like that.

Actually, the Clark Creek Natural Area starts out in a parking lot on a hilltop about 300 feet above sea level, according to a topographical map I looked at later.

The path going in is a steep drop of around ten stories over the first half mile before it ever gets to Clark Creek. I left the path and followed the creek when I finally found it. I knew the creek would wind up at a waterfall. I wasn't too sure exactly where that path might lead or if I could even follow it, it was so steep and elusive in places.

Clark Creek and the streams feeding it have eaten their way Grand Canyon–style down through loess bluffs over a rather large area that is now owned by the state and included in the Natural Area all summed up under the name of Clark Creek. I would have loved to have grown up here. Here are the hideouts and steep climbs and creeks

CLARK CREEK WATERFALL. I'm always amazed by Mississippi waterfalls. Where I grew up in the Delta, water didn't even run fast, much less fall.

and waterfalls and pirates' dens and robbers' roosts for real that we had only in our imaginations as we thrashed through the brush and bar pits behind the levee at Greenville.

From the level of the waterfalls, there is only one way back to the parking lot. Up. Way up. As tough as hiking in had been, now gravity and steep inclines were added.

The climb was so difficult I was beginning to think I might have to homestead down there.

I get about as much exercise as your typical American. The longest walk I take is from the parking lot through Wal-Mart and back to the parking lot. And hey, the trip out to the car is behind a loaded buggy! So I wasn't exactly physically prepared for the long climb at Clark Creek.

On the most impossible rises, some kind souls had built wooden steps. I couldn't imagine how in the world anyone had ever brought that much timber in this far from the parking lot. But I was glad they had, and if I knew who they were, I'd nominate them for sainthood.

But even the wooden steps became a curse after a while. Just when I thought I must be getting close to the top of the hill and the parking lot, I'd round a bend only to find another set of steps there in front of me.

I remember stopping to rest at a tree trunk carved with initials. I wondered if other hikers had time to cut their marks there while waiting for their heart rates to drop back to under 150, as I was doing.

Youngsters have no problem scrambling up and down the hills and gullies at Clark Creek. Someone told me the other day that the last time he was there, there was a school group on a field trip running up and down the paths everywhere. And a teacher was sitting on a log between two hills. She was a rather large woman, he told me. And as she sat she looked at the hill before her and behind her and explained that she was unable to climb either. She was stuck. The driver and several students came back and helped.

CAME THIS WAY. A tree near Clark Creek Falls attests to having had its share of visitors over time with a collection of carved initials.

I was beginning to think I was stuck there, too. After a while, I couldn't manage the goal I had set for myself of walking at least hundred paces before stopping to rest. My spurts of moving were growing shorter, and my rest periods were growing longer. I may never have finished that climb had I not remembered that the area around Clark Creek is one of the last habitats for the black bear in Mississippi. When I thought I could go no farther, I'd hear a rustling in the underbrush and decide to keep moving.

Luckily, time blurs our memory of bad experiences, such as prepping for a colonoscopy or moving to a different house. Sooner or later you forget, and you're ready to try it again.

WATCHING THE WATER. Although the way out is steep and tiring, Clark Creek is usually full of weekend hikers.

Sitting here at the keyboard remembering the stillness of Clark Creek and the remoteness and the water giggling over the rocks and pebbles in the creek bed until it gets to where it rushes off the rock shelf and splashes into the pool below, and the dankness of a hot summer afternoon as the smells of the leaves and dampness permeate the whole creek bed, I think the climb out couldn't have been that bad. And I decide it would be a kick to go back—this time with a lighter camera and maybe one of the grandkids along to carry it.

As you come out of the parking lot at Clark Creek, to the left a few miles is Fort Adams. There's not much left of the town. And there is nothing left of the fort. In Colonial times and before the Louisiana Purchase, Fort Adams was the farthest southwest corner of the nation. To the west across the Mississippi River was the Louisiana Colony owned by France, then Spain, and then France again.

The fort was manned by as many as 500 troops at the height of its importance. But there had been people on the fort hill for hundreds and hundreds of years before the Europeans arrived. The Native Americans used the hill as a ceremonial area, and there was not a tree or a blade of grass growing on it then.

FORT ADAMS is just a quiet village at the end of Highway 24 near the Mississippi River today. But on that hill back of town once stood an important fort.

FORT ADAMS CHIMNEY. This is a still frame of video from a *Look Around Mississippi* story. I just liked the simplicity of the design set off by the January colors of the trees on the hill behind.

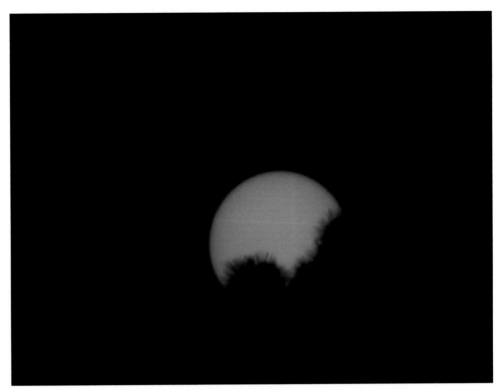

French explorers coming up the Mississippi River held Easter Mass on the hill in 1703. Then Father Antoine Davion, a French priest, came down from Quebec and began a mission there about that time. There is a granite marker erected by the Colonial Dames in his honor on the hilltop. Also, they say this hilltop is really the lower terminus of the Natchez Trace. Makes sense.

When the United States bought Louisiana, suddenly Fort Adams was no longer the frontier beacon for the nation but was just an inland fortification that didn't protect anything in particular anymore and was phased out.

The small town of Fort Adams consists nowadays of a couple of old deserted buildings, one new convenience store, a church or so, several houses, and probably more lore and history than any area its size anywhere else.

The population of Fort Adams swells about a thousand percent every hunting season as an army invades the area and sets up in deer camps to enjoy the bounty of the deep woods and hills and hollows and isolation of Wilkinson County.

Back at Clark Creek, if you were to turn right out of the parking lot, about a quarter of a mile down the road you'd come to Pond, Mississippi. At Pond there is a pond. And across the road from it is the Pond Store. That's it, other than some ducks and geese that live in the pond.

Liz Chaffin runs the store at Pond. Liz has told me a couple of great ghost stories about the place. One of the old owners, Mr. Limkowitz, told Liz's mother and

LONELY SUNSET. Day is dying in the west behind pines and hardwoods. And when you're in the wilderness at sunset you are so much more alone.

father, who worked for him, that after he died, if he could, he wanted to come back from time to time and check on the place. He said not to worry, he wouldn't harm anyone.

Years later when the Chaffin daughters were still young, they ran screaming back into the living quarters from the dark store one night yelling that Mr. Limkowitz was in there.

Liz says she doesn't know what the children saw that night, but even now, decades later, neither of them will go into the store after it is closed and dark.

Maybe the best story has to do with the time the telephone went out and a repairman came to the Pond Store to fix it. Liz said he was directed to the phone back in the living quarters, and in a few minutes he slowly walked into the store, pliers in one hand and wire cutters in the other, asking if they had a ghost there. Liz said, "Well, yes," sort of apologetically. "Well, he's been back here watching me fix the phone," the repairman said.

Liz says that same man still drops by from time to time today.

Liz's mother made a great observation one time when I had stopped into the store and was chatting with her. She told me that when she was a little girl on Saturday mornings they would hitch up the team to the wagon and ride into town, stopping and having coffee with every neighbor along the way. They'd do their shopping and then ride back home that afternoon, stopping again at every neighbor's along the way, and had plenty of time to do everything.

Now, we have cars and clothes washers and clothes dryers and microwave ovens and electric coffee makers and dishwashers and all these other time-saving devices, and yet we don't have time to do anything. What happened?

Kind of makes you wonder why Mr. Limkowitz wants to keep coming back. Unless it's to gloat.

POND STORE was built in 1881. You can usually find maps for the Clark Creek hiking trails here, plus bottled water for the hike.

The seat of territorial history along the river is Woodville, the county seat of Wilkinson County. The Woodville Republican newspaper is Mississippi's oldest continuously operated business. The building housing the Wilkinson County Historical Society used to be the home office for the West Feliciana Railroad, the first standard gauge railroad west of the Appalachians. The Territorial Bank Building still stands in Woodville.

WOODVILLE CHURCH BUILDING. I just love the character of old buildings. New ones are good, too. But I take very few shots of new buildings. I don't know why.

WOODVILLE WIND GAUGE. I was walking on the square at Woodville and happened to glance up and see this atop a building. Kind of interesting, I thought.

TERRITORIAL BANK BUILDING, WOODVILLE. The building was built prior to 1811 and is being transformed into the Wilkinson County African American Museum.

ANCIENT OAKS droop limbs all the way to the ground at the Wilkinson County Courthouse in Woodville.

There are a couple of old ruins in the county. The Union burned Bowling Green Mansion. The family managed to get the piano out before the fire was set. All that's left there now are the brick columns from the front of the house. And there's one fewer of them than used to be. A worker on the place needed some bricks one day and didn't think anyone would mind if he dropped one of the old columns and got the brick from it. After all, it was so old, who'd care?

Sort of the same thing happened at Springfield Plantation on up the river in Jefferson County. Someone needing lumber to repair his mother's home tore down one of the 150-year-old houses in the slave quarters one Saturday morning and hauled the timber away. It was such an old house anyway, who'd care?

They don't make new old history. Once it's gone, it's gone.

BOWLING GREEN was burned by the Yankees in the Civil War. Old columns stand with the oaks in a green meadow where the house once was.

SPRINGFIELD PLANTATION is farther north, near Fayette on Highway 553. Andrew Jackson married Rachel Robards here.

SAINT PAUL'S EPISCOPAL CHURCH, WOODVILLE, is the oldest Episcopal church outside the thirteen original states.

I like the ancient live oaks on the courthouse grounds at Woodville. And I also like the old churches. The Baptist Church worships in the oldest church building in the state. Jefferson Davis' mother was a member of the Episcopal Church.

Jefferson Davis' boyhood home, Rosemont, is at Woodville. Some of the Davis family is buried there.

And as I understand from my own family history, my grandmother Grayson, née Welch, was raised near Woodville before moving to Louisiana and marrying my grandfather.

Immediately after WLBT put up its new tower to replace the one that fell in 1987, the station did a promotion in the fringe areas that had been unable to receive our signal while we were rebuilding. Once a week, we would put Skycopter Three in the air, fly to a town that had not been able to receive us, and do a live shot for our "Noon Newscast" while hovering about 2,000 feet above the town. Then we would set down, shake hands, and greet some folks, shoot some footage, then fly back to Jackson and edit what we'd shot for showing in a later newscast that day.

The last of these fly-ins was to McComb. As we were lifting off to zip straight back up I-55 to Jackson, I told Coyt Bailey, the pilot, that we had been pretty good about going directly to our destinations and then going fairly straight back home so far. He agreed. So I said I wanted to sin a little on our last outing and fly over Woodville and then the Clark Creek Waterfalls before flying back to Jackson.

ROSEMONT PLANTATION VIEW. Out a bedroom window, fall has turned a small dogwood into a salmon-colored still life. The plantation is kept much as it would have looked when it was new.

COZY KITCHEN. A cheery fire warms a damp winter day in the kitchen building at Rosemont Plantation at Woodville.

ROSEMONT PLANTATION was the boyhood home of Jefferson Davis. The house was built in 1810.

WILKINSON COUNTY COURTHOUSE. This is the third courthouse in Woodville, constructed in 1903. The first was a log building.

53

So we changed course and headed west. After we passed Liberty and Centreville, the open meadows and pastures began to fill in with more and more trees until by the time we got to Wilkinson County it looked like a rain forest canopy down below us. Solid woods flowed in all directions. Fall color was beginning to flare in the tops of the hardwoods. So as far as we could see there were orange and red and brown splotches over the whole world until everything got lost in the blue haze of water vapor that shrouds this part of the country out toward the horizon.

Woodville emerged like a jewel out of the mists. Coyt wasn't familiar with Clark Creek, and the only way I could tell him to get there was to follow the highway from Woodville to Pond. Coyt called it flying IFR, "I follow roads."

About that time Skycopter photographer Joe Root spotted some migrating ducks flying south in their "V" formation. Joe asked Coyt if he knew why ducks fly in a "V." Coyt took the opportunity to expound on aerodynamics and lift and drag and wind resistance. "Oh," said Joe when he finished.

Then Joe asked him if he knew why one leg of the "V" was longer than the other. Coyt stuttered a minute and said no, he really didn't. "Why, there's more ducks on one side," finished Joe.

End of flying lesson.

We managed to pick out the ribbon of road as it peeked from the treetops out from Woodville southwest to Pond. And we found the Pond pond okay. Following the creek was a bit more difficult. Coyt nestled Skycopter down below the crest of the hills into the valley. It was the only time while we were doing our fly-ins that you could look out and see hilltops above us.

WOODVILLE has just about the oldest anything in the state located in it or nearby in Wilkinson County.

WILDERNESS WAY. A footpath wanders over the top of a bluff between Fort Adams and Pond. No doubt deer use the path, followed by hunters.

CLEAR SKIES show through a break in the canopy of trees on a back road in Wilkinson County.

We crept through the valley watching for signs of the stream. Joe Root saw it first and trained his remote camera mounted under the helicopter on the clearing in the trees above one of the waterfalls, and Coyt slowly circled the spot as Joe rolled video-tape on the area.

Up above, we rolled tape as we followed the valley until it widened out where it met the Mississippi River. Beyond, we could clearly see the locks on the Louisiana side where the Red River flows into the Mississippi just across the river from Fort Adams.

But it was the remoteness of Wilkinson County that struck me most looking down on it from above. We'd cross a highway every now and again, but it would be completely flanked by deep woods on either side.

Someone from Woodville told me that the population of Wilkinson County at the time of the Civil War was about 2,000. He said the population of Wilkinson County since then up until the present has been no more than plus or minus a hundred people of that same figure.

It's not that there is no progress there, there just has been no influx of people. It remains remote out in the countryside. And Woodville has remained a quaint county seat and not bothered to try to turn itself into a tourist magnet, which is what attracts tourists there and has attracted retirees from places like New Orleans to come settle in the area. It's just like it always has been with the natural progression of the times. But no unnatural progression of the times.

Traveling northward up Highway 61 from Woodville and Wilkinson County, you find where some British Loyalists settled in this part of the country around the outbreak of the Revolutionary War. One of the first places you come across inside Adams County is Kingston, also known as the Jersey Settlement because most of its original population came from the New Jersey area of the mid-Atlantic coast.

CROWN GLASS RIPPLES. The old windowpanes were made when molten glass was poured onto a flat surface and then cut to shape after it hardened. Imperfections give it character.

The oldest Protestant congregation in the state still holds weekly worship services at Kingston Methodist Church. Their building, however, was constructed in the mid-1800s, so it is not as old as the Woodville Baptist Church building.

We did a *Look Around* story at the church last year when the pastor, Lou Knighton, gave me a call and said the church was in kind of a fix. The Kingston congregation has shrunk to a size just about minimal to maintain the everyday expenses of running a country church. The problem is the church building is on the National Register of Historic Places and needs repair.

More than a century and a half of Mississippi heat and humidity has the original plaster on the sanctuary walls turning to chalk and crumbling. And when you have plaster chunking off nationally registered walls built ca. 1850, you can't just hop down to Home Depot and get a load of plywood and cover it. You can't even mix a little plaster and fix it yourself. And hiring experts in nineteenth-century restoration is a little out of the league of a struggling country church.

I guess this is where culture meets culture shock. Maybe the descendants who return for the annual homecoming service every spring at Kingston Methodist can help.

Speaking of homecoming services, I had to preach one a few summers ago at Sarepta United Methodist Church in rural Claiborne County. I had been invited to come do a story about the service and had notified the church to be expecting me.

KINGSTON CHURCH in Adams County has roots that run back to Colonial times. The church meets in this mid-1800s building.

Sarepta is one of those churches whose congregation has dwindled to the point that they no longer have regular services but still open the doors once a year for a homecoming.

A former pastor had been invited to speak that day. He was now the pastor of a church up in the Delta. When he found out I was going to be there, he phoned me and explained he had a building committee meeting scheduled for the same day he was scheduled to preach at Sarepta. He realized it would be rather difficult to preach in Claiborne County, then eat, and still make that meeting and asked if I didn't mind, would I just go ahead and deliver the message that day since I was going to be there anyway.

Now the reason he invited me to fill the pulpit for him is that I am an ordained Baptist minister. I pastored a small church way up in the northern part of Madison County when I was a student at Mississippi College. I didn't pursue a career in ministry. But for Baptists, as with our salvation, once ordained, always ordained.

A quick story: Being ordained, I can marry people but choose not to. I feel marrying folks is the role of the minister of the couple involved as a part of his charge to minister to families, especially brand-new ones. The very last wedding I performed was that of my daughter and son-in-law. (And I was their second choice!)

Several years ago, however, one of the girls in the newsroom wanted me to perform her wedding, and she just wouldn't have it any other way. So the night came, and I stepped up and acted in the role of minister and did the ceremony. Afterwards, a lady who knew me from watching me do weather on WLBT walked up to me with a puzzled look on her face and asked me how it was that I could perform a wedding. I told her that in Mississippi weathermen could legally marry folks, then turned and walked away.

So I told the former Sarepta pastor that I didn't mind filling in for him, but I explained to him that it had been a long time since I had preached. He said it didn't matter; the people wouldn't be coming to hear my sermon anyway. They came for dinner on the grounds.

A few days before I was to preach that weekend, I took my daughter, Keri, to lunch, and she asked me what I intended to preach about. I told her I had about

WOODVILLE BAPTIST CHURCH is the oldest church building in the state. It was built in 1809.

zeroed in on the Four Commandments. Four? There are ten, she reminded me. I told her I realized that, but I was only comfortable talking about four of them anymore.

Keri went on telling me that Jesus said that if you so much as hated your brother it was the same as having killed him. Her point was, I may not be as comfortable with even those four commandments as I thought I might be. Had I even thought of breaking any of them, I was deemed as guilty as if I had. (That's one way to shorten a sermon.) I told her she was right.

So I preached on forgiveness. I told the congregation how I had arrived at the topic for the morning, relating the story about the discussion with my daughter over lunch. Then, after the service had ended, Gordon Cotton, the curator of the Old Courthouse Museum in Vicksburg, came up to me to say hello.

Gordon told me that sometimes he is called on to fill the pulpit at his Primitive Baptist church south of Vicksburg. Gordon said he had a "damn Yankee" from Ohio staying with him one summer while doing Civil War research at the Old Courthouse. Gordon was to preach the following Sunday.

That Saturday night Gordon was going over his notes when his guest asked Gordon his topic. "I am going to preach on forgiveness," Gordon said.

"Forgiveness!" shouted the Ohioan, "Forgiveness!" His voice pitched higher. "What do you Southerners know about forgiveness? Until you can forgive Sherman for his March to the Sea, you have no right to even think about forgiveness."

Gordon said, "So I changed my topic."

Near the turn to Kingston is an icon of Highway 61, Mammy's Cupboard, constructed back in the day when it was popular to build buildings that suggested their use. For instance, there have been diners shaped like hot dogs. The first Brown Derby restaurant in California was actually shaped like a hat. In Massachusetts there's a restaurant shaped like both a milk can and another like a milk bottle.

Well, Mammy's Cupboard is a restaurant shaped like an old Southern Negro cook. Lots of people have taken offense at Mammy over the years. But in the day and age when she was built, she wasn't intended to offend. She sort of reminds me of the affection felt between white families and their maids and domestic help back then—a sort of

DINNER ON THE GROUNDS at the annual Homecoming Sunday is always good no matter the quality of the sermon preceding it.

OLD TIME RELIGION is not hard to come by in the Lower River Country of southwest Mississippi. There are old churches scattered all over out here.

family bond that really happened in that era. I don't know that those bonds are understood today. And they certainly wouldn't be P.C. anymore because of changing cultural conditions.

Back when I was growing up, we had a maid at our house. There were five kids in our family. Of course, by the time the youngest was born, the oldest two had already married and left. But there were plenty of folks on hand all the time in between. And Grandpa Grayson lived with us, too, another mouth to cook for and more clutter to be picked up after.

Mama didn't have a job outside the house in those days except for a short stint selling Avon cosmetics at Broadway Cleaners in Greenville every Saturday (pay-day) for a while. Most days she'd come home and just sob because instead of augmenting Daddy's income, she'd have to foot the bill for late-pays. I don't know if she ever came out ahead.

At that time in Greenville there weren't many opportunities for women wanting to have a career of any sort. Women were clerks in department stores, were secretaries for businessmen, or could do fairly menial jobs such as working at the cleaners. A tiny number of women had real careers as physicians or journalists but not many. I don't remember any female lawyers.

A bright, college-educated, outgoing woman who needed or wanted to work usually became a schoolteacher, a position of some respect in those long–ago days, or a nurse, a profession that Mama longed to join but for which she had had no chance to receive any training. So, like most women in her generation, she stayed home and took care of the family and was helped by black women who had even fewer economic opportunities.

Mama cooked three brand-new hot meals every day of the week, including Sunday. And washed and hung out laundry and ironed and cleaned and entertained various groups from the church and took food for funerals and had relatives and friends in and out of the house all day. So with all the people living in our house, she needed help.

So Clara came into our home. She stayed for years until all of us children, and even her own grandchildren, were grown and gone. She lived a few streets over from us in the easy, helter-skelter way that white and black neighborhoods abutted one another back then. Clara not only lifted some of the load off mama but took it upon herself to add to her job description by scolding us kids when we needed it and in

MAMMY'S CUPBOARD still serves lunch every day. Enter through the hoop skirt into a large dining room beyond.

general helped raise us, too. She added to the mix of grownups who were always there, figuratively and even more important, physically, for us children.

One of my sisters can still remember vividly the only day in her childhood that she ever came home to our house and it was empty. No one was there. She sat down in the middle of the living room floor and cried, fearing some calamity must have occurred for Grandpa to be gone from the living room and Clara to be missing from the kitchen.

Recently my wife, Jo, and I went to visitation for the son of a friend who passed away suddenly. In the line of well-wishers behind us was a black family. As we were talking to the mother of the deceased, she pointed out that these people were the children of the maid who worked for her family for years and had helped her raise her children. They were like family.

The mom went on to say that when the maid passed away several years ago, in her obituary not only were her own children listed as survivors but also the white mom for whom she had worked and her kids. And that's kind of the way it was.

We've come a long way since the days of my childhood in race relations, in economic opportunity, and in opportunities for women. We meet today as equals, and it's better this way. But we can still salute the good that was there in the old days and old ways, and we can realize again that our future here depends on mutual understanding and willingness to go forward together.

So Mammy is a reflection of a tradition of Southern culture that to me actually lifts her up as sort of a guardian and an adopted family member—an adoption that went both ways—as her real-life counterparts were thought of. Instead of taking offense by interpreting a seventy-year-old relic as if it had been conceived of today, celebrate Mammy for what it is, an icon in brick and

SIR WILLIAM DUNBAR, planter, scientist, and friend of President Jefferson, is buried at The Forest Plantation south of Natchez.

plaster of the last idealized era of the South, an age that, even though not perfect, was perceived as being so.

Nearby on Highway 61 south of Natchez is the historic marker for The Forest, one of the old plantations in the area. The only surviving parts of the house are the columns that supported the upper gallery on the front, and the cemetery.

William Dunbar is buried in the cemetery at The Forest. He was a planter, a scientist, and a good friend of Thomas Jefferson. Dunbar was one of the first to traipse out West and explore the Louisiana Purchase. Lewis and Clark got most of the press, however.

Earlier, Dunbar was hired by Spain as their representative when President Washington ordered a survey of the 31st parallel. That was the dividing line between the territory belonging to the brand-new USA to the north and the Spanish colony of West Florida to the south. It is the state line between Louisiana and Mississippi today south of Woodville. Dunbar said Andrew Ellicott's company, the representatives commissioned by Washington surveying for the United States, placed the line some one hundred yards too far to the north. Getting it even that close sounds pretty accurate to me when you figure you are sighting off the constellations to begin with.

If you go to the tour home Longwood in Natchez, you will see wooden crates on display there that once contained furniture with stenciled addresses on them sent to Julia Nutt at The Forest. Furnishings for the grand home Longwood started arriving while the Nutt family was scattered about living here and there with friends and relatives while Longwood was being built.

RIVER REEDS. A little sunlight manages to filter through the surrounding trees to dapple a stand of reeds growing in a creek bottom out in the wilderness.

GOLDEN YEARS. Mississippi, not having mountainsides, isn't known all that well for fall color. But individual trees put on shows where they can.

GRAPES OF SPRING. Wisteria hangs like bunches of grapes, trained onto trellises in yards, and naturally drapes over entire hillsides where old houses once were.

WILDERNESS WATERFALL. This is just the kind of surprise that makes taking a nature trail worth the hike. There are many places like this creek and waterfall in the Lower River Country.

Natchez

AND CEMETERY STORIES

I GUESS THE FIRST TIME I EVER HEARD OF NATCHEZ was in association with Longwood. My third-grade teacher took a weekend trip to Natchez and came back to our classroom in Greenville the next Monday, telling us all about the town and the river and especially Longwood.

She said there was this unusual octagon-shaped house that was being built at the time the Civil War started. The Northern workers commissioned to build it put down their tools and left after they got word of the firing on Fort Sumter, trying to reach their homes up North before borders were sealed and battle lines drawn. She told us that to this day, their tools were still lying right where they were dropped a hundred years earlier when the workers fled Longwood and Natchez. The idea that something someone had touched as long ago as the Civil War was still lying right where it was left was thrilling to me.

Over time, Longwood became one of my favorite destinations for *Looking Around* stories. There was always another good tale at Longwood. The then-manager of Longwood, Mrs. Burns, and I got to be good friends before her retirement. She was the resident manager; she lived there by herself in that big, empty house.

The Natchez Pilgrimage Garden Club has owned the house since the 1960s, has restored the grounds, and keeps Longwood open as a tour home on a daily basis.

Ever since those days at WJPR with its knocking walls, I'd been a fan of ghosts and ghost stories. So one day I asked Mrs. Burns if Longwood was haunted. "Yes," she answered, and went on to tell me the story of how one night in her bed her head

LONGWOOD. Dr. Haller Nutt and his wife, Julia, were building this house when the Civil War started. It is just a shell. Only the basement floor inside was completed.

was lifted up off the pillow and turned from side to side and then lowered back down by unseen hands.

I asked Mrs. Burns if she minded if I mentioned the ghosts in some of my stories to run on the air. "I don't mind at all," she told me. "Having people think the place is haunted saves money on security."

Longwood is like Windsor in the sense I'd have loved to have seen both of them completed. Windsor, of course, will never be rebuilt, and Longwood will never be finished. Longwood will forever remain a shell. It's the essence of the Old South after the Civil War—just a facade.

I had been to Natchez just one time before I started making regular trips there to do *Look Around Mississippi* stories. Many years earlier when I was working at WRBC radio in Jackson, our station manager was marrying the traffic girl (traffic people were the ones who scheduled the commercials), and I had been asked to participate in the ceremony. (This was way before I was ordained; they just wanted me to read something.)

They were married in St. Mary's Cathedral. That was so long ago that I really don't remember much about it except I was allowed to sit in the Bishop's Chair. They had me read Paul's exhortation on love from First Corinthians 13.

I remember the church was beautiful. The sanctuary was surrounded with stained glass windows, and there were statues everywhere. And the high ceiling made it seem cavernous, especially compared with the small church I was raised in.

St. Mary's was built right on top of Natchez's first community burial ground. The bodies of those whose remains were not identifiable were put into a common burial under the floor, and the church was built over them. Most of the graves were relocated to the current Natchez City Cemetery in about 1822.

The first time I went to Natchez City Cemetery was a midsummer afternoon when twilight lasts a good while. I got there about 5:30 p.m. so it would be late enough for the shadows to be long but early enough to have plenty of light left to shoot video.

There are about 10,000 people buried there. And that means there are 10,000 good stories.

ST. MARY'S, NATCHEZ, is still known as the cathedral, even though the seat of diocesan administration has been moved to Jackson. However, now minor basilica status has been bestowed on St. Mary's.

Twelve-year-old Rosalie Beekman is buried there. She was the only battle casualty of the Civil War in Natchez. A Union gunboat pulled up in the Mississippi River at the foot of the city and demanded ice. Nobody in Natchez was all that interested in selling or giving ice to them, so the boat began shelling Natchez Under the Hill where the Beekmans ran a dry-goods store.

Mr. Beekman gathered his family together and started them running up the bluff toward the town proper to get away, but a shell exploded nearby, and a piece of shrapnel caught Rosalie across the back of the leg and cut an artery.

As she stumbled and fell, her father yelled for her to get up and run. "I can't," cried little Rosalie. "I've been kilt."

There is another child, Irene Washington, who has a set of steps behind her headstone that goes all the way down to the coffin level of her grave. She died in the late 1800s at about ten years of age. Irene was afraid of storms. The steps were installed so her mother could go to the cemetery and sit with Irene every time thunder and lightning started.

One of the saddest tombstones has just three words on it. But those three words encompass as much as entire books. It reads, "Louise," on the top line. And under it, "The Unfortunate."

Not only is the cemetery full of stories about the people buried there; to me the statuary and the iron fences around burial plots should be in a museum somewhere, not sprawled out weathering on a hillside.

So Natchez City Cemetery seemed like a great place to go to get a *Look Around Mississippi* story. As I wheeled through the gate, I noticed a sign posted on the side that said, "Gates closed at 7 p.m." Well, it was just 5:30. That would give me an hour and a half. And it wasn't like I was going to have to chase anybody down. All the subjects I came to shoot were pretty much where they were going to be.

So I got started looking for the graves of people like Rosalie Beekman and the Barber of Natchez, the freeman who lived here before the Civil War and left a diary full of gossip he'd overheard while cutting hair.

IRENE WASHINGTON GRAVE, NATCHEZ, has a set of concrete steps descending behind the headstone. The window has been sealed off so you can no longer see the coffin inside.

And I was also intrigued with the marble works and the fences and the epitaphs on the tombstones. I got so carried away, I forgot to check my watch until I was way over in the back part of the cemetery and glanced down and saw that it was ten minutes after seven.

Well, gates close at seven, I figured I could always just open the gate and drive on out. Now, if they had added just one line to the closing notice on the sign at the gatepost to make it read, "Gates closed and **locked** at 7 p.m.," I'd have paid a lot more attention to the time.

Here I was on the wrong side of a locked gate, in a cemetery, of all places, and it was getting on toward 7:20 p.m. by now, and I had to be back in Jackson in a coat and tie on the set at WLBT doing 10 p.m. weather in less than three hours. I had my cell phone and called the Natchez Police. The dispatcher told me not to worry, this happened all the time. He gave me the phone number of a man who lived across the street from the cemetery who had a key just for such instances.

Great! I punched the number into my phone. Ring, ring, ring, ring. Click. "Hello! We're not in this evening, but if you'll leave your name and number, we'll get back to you as soon as we can."

Now I was in a panic. I left my name and asked that they please check the cemetery when they got back, and if I was still in there, bring a couple of sandwiches and a key!

As I drove from gate to gate to see if they had overlooked locking just one of them, I ran across a couple of joggers. I asked them how I could get out. They told me I couldn't. "You're stuck in here until morning."

I want you to know that five minutes later, I was back in downtown Natchez making the left turn from Canal onto Franklin, heading back to Highway 61 and toward Jackson. All the incentive I needed to get out was just being told I would have to spend the night in a cemetery.

LOUISE THE UNFORTUNATE. No doubt many a mother has dragged her children-going-bad out to the cemetery to see this headstone as a warning to change their ways.

NATCHEZ DOWNTOWN is a lively mix of shops, restaurants, and offices. This is a video still from a *Look Around Mississippi* story.

NATCHEZ CITY CEMETERY, NIGHT. Once a year, the Angels on the Bluff evening tour has people acting out the parts of the departed as they stand over their headstones. This is a still video shot from a *Look Around Mississippi* story.

I'm not sure how I managed to get out. But I figure next morning the groundskeeper probably wondered why the crape myrtles that used to grow by the fence were farther apart than they used to be.

Now, skip forward a few years until just after Jo and I married. Jo was my junior high school sweetheart back in Greenville. We were each other's first love. When I went on to high school, Jo being a year younger and still in junior high, I figured I had outgrown her. So we let that relationship cool for about thirty-five years, during which time we were married to other people.

Well, Jo and I kept up with each other over the years with Christmas cards and a phone call every few years. And (simple version) Jo and I hit bumps in our marriages about the same time and wound up back together.

But things had changed. Jo had a family now. And her daughter and son-in-law and the kids moved to Jackson along with Jo. I figured we needed a family outing so these folks could get to know who this guy was who had married Mom.

So we went to Natchez. We ate fried chicken at the Carriage House Restaurant, toured Stanton Hall and Longwood, and were about to head back home when I remembered Natchez City Cemetery. I snapped my fingers and told the group we had to go see my favorite place in Natchez before we left. And between downtown Natchez and the cemetery, I told them the story about how I got locked in the first time I went there.

STANTON HALL, NATCHEZ. Natchez was home to more millionaires than any other city in the nation prior to the Civil War. Here's how the banker lived.

NATCHEZ CITY CEMETERY AZALEAS are bright patches of color in the spring. In addition, there are many antique rose varieties in the cemetery, some found nowhere else in the country.

As we were going in the gate, our son-in-law, Brad, made the comment that it was getting awfully late now. I told him not to worry about getting locked in again. "Lightning never strikes twice in the same place." And we rolled on.

All I wanted to do was drive through so they could get a quick peek. So we went over the hill into the hollow on the other side. Made the left-hand turn that took us back to the exit road. Turned left on it and drove back over the crest of the hill, and drove up to a locked gate!

I was stunned. The rest of the family was in stitches laughing. I couldn't believe it. I got out of the car and walked over toward the gate. Maybe the lock was just hung there and not snapped.

About that time, a man in a coat and tie (it was Sunday night) came out of a house across the street and saw the car inside the gate. Realizing our situation, he yelled, "Oh, y'all are locked in. Hang on, I have the key...." Then looking closer at us, he yelled, "Walt! Is that you again?"

Not too long ago, Don Estes, director of the cemetery, took Jo and me on a guided tour of his burial grounds, and when he finished, asked how we liked the place. I told him I liked it so much that I had been locked in twice. He told us to wait a minute and went back into his office. Returning, he started to hand me a key but hesitated because I obviously could be the poster boy for idiots after being locked in to begin with, much less twice. So Don gave Jo the key. It fits the padlock on the gate. And Don told us that from now on, we could come and go as we pleased.

Natchez is an endless fascination to me. I have to make myself not go to Natchez and do stories so my segment won't end up being called *Looking Around Natchez.*

But since we are in a cemetery, let's visit another one at a picturesque country church right up the road from Natchez in Jefferson County, Church Hill.

I was trying to remember how I first heard of Church Hill. Maybe it was listed in the WPA *Guide to Mississippi* published during the Depression years. I have a paperback reprint of that book and have culled stories from time to time. Or I could have just wandered down Highway 553 taking a long-cut to Natchez and stumbled upon it.

Church Hill is exactly that, a church on a hill. It was one of those places settled by English loyalist refugees from the mid-Atlantic region around the time of the Revolutionary War. It is also known as the Maryland Community.

Christ Episcopal Church on the hill at Church Hill was built in 1857. They still hold regular services every third Sunday of the month. But the building is open pretty much all the time.

The first time I went there to do a story, the Wagoners, who ran the old store across the road, let me in and showed me around. One of the interesting things I found out is that there is a grave under the church. The story goes that while the church was under construction, the wife of the pastor died. It was her wish to be buried beneath the pulpit.

CHURCH HILL DAYLILY. This daylily bloom lasted only a day, in contrast to its location, an area of the state that is ancient by Mississippi standards.

CHURCH HILL WINDOW. A cascade of color fills the sanctuary at Christ Church when the sun gets just right.

On the east side of the building there is a door leading down to a cramped basement below, made even more cramped with a relatively modern furnace down there. The lip of the basement is just a little over head-high, so you have to stand on your tiptoes to see over the edge of it. And there is no light under the rest of the church except for the little bit that seeps in through the iron vent grates in the brick wall. And the basement is down toward the middle of the building, while the pulpit is toward one end. So it is pretty difficult to really see anything all the way up in the pulpit area from the basement.

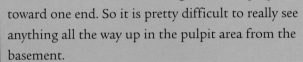

But I was assured there was a grave and grave marker there in the shadows. So I plopped my camera up over the ledge and steadied it on the top of the ground beneath the church and zoomed my lens as tight as I could and hiked up the gain to make the darkness under the church a little brighter and caught something white in my viewfinder. I rolled tape on it and called it a grave when I showed it on the air.

My only salvation is the fuzzy image of whatever I shot under the church that day and captured on videotape and called a grave can't be disproved.

Church Hill is another of those places Eudora Welty photographed in the 1930s and 1940s. She was such a fan of cemeteries that she could have been a member of my family. Our people, especially on my mother's side, have a fascination with death. My brother, David, is the keeper of the family skeletons. He can tell you who of our ancestors died where and when.

While Mama was living, we'd phone her at home in Fulton now and again to check on her and see how she was doing and if she needed anything. And we'd have hardly said hello before she'd start calling the roll of who all had passed away since last we talked. Then she'd try to get us to remember them, trying to think of places where ours and the deceased's paths may have crossed. "You know, you saw them at church that Sunday you were here at Christmas in 1989. They sat three pews behind us." To which we would finally feign enlightenment and utter an "Oh, yeah" so the conversation could progress.

CHRIST CHURCH, CHURCH HILL is another quaint old country churchyard. There are several antebellum plantation homes nearby, some of which are B&Bs, on Highway 553 in Jefferson County.

The dying became such a part of living back in Fulton that one time when my brother, Robert, from Memphis popped down for the weekend, he tongue-in-cheek asked Mama who was showing down at the funeral home.

The churchyard at Church Hill is old and yet new, too. There are ancient stones in there from the early 1800s. Monuments of all shapes and sizes in memory of the ones buried beneath them. And new markers, too, not more than a few years old.

A modern young person who left this life all too soon is buried at Church Hill. He has whirligigs and Mardi Gras beads on his grave and a bumper sticker on his tomb stone. That's the saddest one there. He's not here anymore to kid around with, so about the best his friends can do now is kid around with his grave.

And what a sobering thought when someone close to you passes away; now they have a grave. That was a shock to me after Mama died. After we buried her, one corner of her grave started sinking in. I called my brothers and sisters and asked them what to do. Then it hit me: my Mama has a grave.

Eudora Welty made a lot of photographs of the tombs and the church at Church Hill. Over time, so have I. And I have also found some of the other cemeteries she shot during her trips up and down the Natchez Trace and in Crystal Springs and Utica, all the way back to Jackson. I guess this is a good place to talk about some other cemeteries.

Rocky Springs was a popular Eudora Welty cemetery. It isn't all that far up the Natchez Trace from Church Hill. You have to pass through Port Gibson to get to it. But since I intend to spend a whole chapter on Port Gibson pretty quickly, we'll skip over that town for the moment.

The historic markers at Rocky Springs explain it was a pretty sizable and thriving community when the Natchez Trace was in use, before the land washed out from under the town and the surrounding countryside because of poor farming practices.

CHURCH HILL CEMETERY has many interesting old stones. The cemetery was one of Eudora Welty's photographic destinations.

MS. EUDORA'S GRAVE now sits near many of her photographic subjects in Jackson.

As the land yawned into gullies, the people drifted to other areas. The sign at the parking lot at the beginning of the footpath to Rocky Springs off the Natchez Trace explains the town had a population of better than 2,000 people in 1860. The population in 1960 was zero. Not gone with the wind but gone with the soil washed away by the water.

Other than a deserted safe missing its door lying over in the woods, the only thing left of Rocky Springs now to prove a community was ever there is the Methodist Church and the church's cemetery.

They still hold services at the church. I've been to church there a couple of times. Well, one time to Sunday service and another for a wedding. And I've popped my head in the door and looked around a number of times in between when no one was there but me. I've heard ghost stories about the church and try to catch one for myself, I guess. Or I just try to escape reality and run away into the past for a minute. I have a few still shots of the old rippled glass in the windows of Rocky Springs Church. One hangs over my desk in my office at WLBT. It's always good to look up from phone messages and be able to gaze out the window of Rocky Springs Church into the woods beyond.

The first time I went to a church service there was the morning after a campout experience with my friend Kirk Hill and his wife, Rita, and a bunch of their friends in their Model T club. Kirk and Rita sleep out in tents or under the stars all the time. My idea of roughing it is black-and-white television.

ROCKY SPRINGS' PRESENT POPULATION isn't going anywhere, unless unchecked erosion starts again. The cemetery was another favorite of Eudora Welty and her camera.

SO GOES THE WORLD. A geologist told me one time that all nature is trying to do is wash us back into the sea. Erosion at Rocky Springs is testament to that. Still video frame from a *Look Around* story.

Around the campfire that night, I finally did sort of lose myself and forget what it was I wanted to forget by coming camping to begin with. As the clouds cleared and the rain stopped and the temperatures dropped, the campfire roared and thawed us and dried us, and we started telling stories. I actually enjoyed it.

Soon the stories primed us to the point where we wanted adventure. So someone grabbed a coal oil lantern and dared the rest of us to hike the Old Trace from the campground to the cemetery at Rocky Springs Church.

There are times I'd love to see a ghost. Its has never been "right now," however. Sort of like a tornado. I've always wanted to see one. But whenever I get caught in a violent thunderstorm that could actually spawn one, I don't want it to be now! But I was beginning to think the time and the place for a ghostly manifestation had come together as we wandered toward the graveyard in the dark and the cold that night.

Did you know the wind moans louder through treetops at night just after late autumn cold fronts pass when you are walking in the dark woods and you aren't the one holding the lantern? You never notice moaning wind when you are at home at night in your living room watching television, flipping channels trying to find out what else is on besides *Fear Factor*. But you become quite aware of it as the shapes of the tombstones of a forlorn cemetery come into view in the dim moonlight way after dark. Especially after everyone splits up, and the person who is holding the lantern goes the other way.

Under the quarter moon, shadows duck and hide behind the stone fences that surround individual family plots. And they dash silently through the underbrush and tease behind the tombstones. And you wish you were about ten years old again so you could actually believe all of this stuff you are trying so hard to convince your-

HAUNTING THE CEMETERY with a lantern at night can be fun, especially if you are the one holding the lantern. I wasn't.

VIEW FROM THE BLUFF. The high ground at Natchez City Cemetery is a favored burial place above the Mississippi River flood plain below.

self is really happening so you could really get as scared as you are trying to make yourself. Sometimes a good fear is just the factor you need to overcome reality that is scary and you wish wasn't as real as it was.

But the cemetery at Rocky Springs after dark on a cold, clearing night with the moon and the north wind is a good diversion anyway, if not an out-and-out escape. However, I don't think you are supposed to be in there after dark. So if you try it and get caught, don't say I ever said it was okay to be there.

But cemeteries are there for the living anyway. And maybe all the statues and carved stones help us forget that dead people are collected here. And maybe it also helps us ignore the inevitability that we will contribute to the quaintness of some cemetery ourselves someday. We can look at the stones and think of the people under them as if their personalities have somehow been transformed into the wonderful markers set above them.

It's those wonderful markers that give character to cemeteries.

Oak Grove Cemetery is in the Ratliff community in Itawamba County. There are six generations of my family buried in Oak Grove, including some from my generation. We've already started burying cousins.

There are a few unusual things in Oak Grove. One of them is a grave shelter. Grave shelters used to be fairly common in some parts of the state, especially in the Piney Woods from, say, Collins south towards New Augusta. But there's at least one in Itawamba County.

Inside the little white house with a door and a window is buried someone from my family who died over a hundred years ago. And although the building doesn't look like it's nearly that old, my Aunt Coleen, who is ninety, says she can't remember a time in her life that it wasn't there.

All sorts of things show up on tombstones. Symbols of where the person hopefully ended up after death. Clouds and angels and heavenly stuff. Preachers often have grave markers shaped like pulpits. Masons have a whole array of symbols on their markers. But only if they were high enough in the order to impress other Masons.

OAK GROVE CEMETERY, ITAWAMBA COUNTY. My forefathers camped on this hilltop while helping to force Cherokees west along the Trail of Tears and then came back and settled in the area. Many are buried here.

GRAVE SHELTER, OAK GROVE. The house over the grave has been there as long as the oldest people in the community can remember.

WOODMAN'S GRAVE. I find it interesting the things people choose for their grave markers. It's like your one last vanity tag, and it has to say a lot.

ON UP THERE. Cryptic Masonic symbols decorate the headstone of someone who attained many levels in the organization. Be impressed. But it's a secret as to why.

GREENWOOD CEMETERY, JACKSON, was a favorite photographic spot for Ms. Welty. There is still a lot of character (and characters) in here.

DELTA PIONEER, GREENVILLE CEMETERY. Looks like a hands-on kind of guy.

I saw one stone in Vicksburg shaped like a piano, obviously over the grave of a musician. Woodmen of the World must have had at least a hundred different configurations of trees and felled logs they could select for their final resting place.

Many people chose something of their lives to represent them in death. In Meridian, near the graves of the Gypsy King and Queen, there is a tombstone with a locomotive on it. In Greenville Cemetery, there is the representation of a stump carved in marble with wood tools on top of it.

Back at Oak Grove, my Granddaddy Cummings' grave marker is a petrified stump. Granddaddy worked in the wood business all his life. When he was younger, he surveyed timber in the Smoky Mountains. Later, he owned sawmills in West Point and on Bull Mountain Creek south of Fulton.

One day Granddaddy dragged home this hunk of petrified wood he had found out in the woods up in Itawamba County somewhere and put it at the end of the front porch. He told Grandmother that he intended to use it as his tombstone. She didn't pay much attention until one day a stonemason came to the house and attached a nameplate with Granddaddy's name and birth date on the stump.

Granddaddy told Grandmother as she watched that since he had worked in wood all his life, it was only fitting that his tombstone somehow represent that. Grandmother wiped her hands on her apron as she turned to go back to the kitchen and told Granddaddy, "Well, if that's the case, then when I die, you can just take the door off the oven and put it over my grave."

JEFFERSON COLLEGE, ADAMS COUNTY, is home of the famous Burr Oaks under which Aaron Burr was supposedly tried for treason. Only he was never tried here. Nor were the oaks even there at the time. Good story otherwise.

GRANDDADDY'S GRAVE at Oak Grove is marked by a stump of petrified wood. He wanted something symbolic of his life as his headstone.

EUDORA'S FADED FLOWERS have almost dissolved over the decades since she photographed them in Jackson's Greenwood Cemetery. They were crisp in her photographs. The years fade even concrete.

We were shooting the stand-ups for *Mississippi Roads* in Jackson one Sunday morning a few years ago. Our producer, Key Ivy, had selected Greenwood Cemetery just off North West Street as a location for one of the story introductions we needed to videotape.

Our regular audio technician, Donald Thomas, wasn't with us that morning. He was out at Tougaloo College preparing the sound equipment for Bill Clinton's visit later that day (the former president was in town to address the students at graduation). As a replacement, Donald arranged for a friend of his from New Orleans to come up and help us.

I love Greenwood Cemetery for the character of its markers and the breadth of its occupants: blacks, whites, rich, poor, powerful, famous, and just folks.

Someday maybe Greenwood Cemetery will be safer to visit again. But it's kind of iffy right now. When the movie crews were shooting the graveyard scenes for Willy Morris' *My Dog Skip* in Greenwood Cemetery one night, there were shots fired at the movie lights from the neighborhood nearby.

So here we were early one Sunday morning hoping to get in and out before the area awoke. The crew was setting up for me to deliver a line or two into the camera introducing a story for an upcoming *Mississippi Roads* show.

We crept into the cemetery and drove all the way down to the turnaround loop and quietly parked our ETV van right behind a little white Toyota pickup truck. It struck me as being a little odd that there was anyone else already in the cemetery that early.

As Key and photographer Randy Kwan were setting up the camera and the substitute audit technician was untangling wires, suddenly out from behind a large grave marker scooted this middle-aged white guy. Dodging us, he slipped into the Toyota truck and hurriedly left. I thought he may have been putting flowers on his mother's grave before church or something like that.

No more than thirty seconds later, out from behind the same grave marker came a young black man wearing a long red dress. Knowing we were there but not acknowledging us, he looked neither left nor right but dashed in a straight line across the graveyard and disappeared through a hole in the hedgerow onto Lamar Street and was absorbed by the neighborhood.

We were all sort of caught in suspended motion for a second, frozen in shock. Finally, our audio man spoke up and thawed us again saying, "Man, I'm from New Orleans, and that's even weird to me!"

I don't think seeing a ghost would have stunned us more. And considering the mental motion picture of the event that replays at will in my brain from time to time, I'd rather it had been a ghost.

I told you cemeteries were for the living.

ROCKING AWAY TIME. A man is buried sitting in a rocking chair in Natchez City Cemetery entombed in this miniature pyramid.

EMERALD MOUND is the second largest Indian mound in the nation. It is associated with the Natchez tribe, wiped out by French colonists in 1729.

Port Gibson

AND RELATED TALES

FROM CHURCH HILL WE DRIVE BACK OUT TO HIGHWAY 61. Nowadays most of the towns along Highway 61 have been bypassed. In addition to creating bypasses, the Department of Transportation is widening the whole road to four lanes from Tennessee to Louisiana.

I read someone's account of driving southward years ago on the old 61 through the southwest Mississippi bluffs below Port Gibson. They wrote of a narrow winding road rising over ridge tops and diving into creek bottoms. The road was lined with ancient oaks laden with Spanish moss that draped all the way to the ground like old men's beards. And the moss swayed with the breeze and cast a sleepy spell over drivers as if they were motoring through a gateway into some enchanted kingdom.

'Tain't that way no more.

Now the right-of-way is as wide and as featureless as an interstate in most places. There are hardly any trees of any age near the road at all, much less ancient oaks. Gone are the kudzu-covered hills and road banks. I'm sure the kudzu will grow back, however. Nothing stops kudzu. Not even progress.

One stormy December night a long time ago, I had been to Natchez shooting the Christmas decorations at Longwood and was driving back to Jackson after dark. The rain was pouring in sheets by the time I got to old Highway 61. In those days before it was widened and four-laned, the kudzu slunk up the guy wires that steadied power poles at the tops of the bluffs and then snaked out on the power lines themselves, giving the illusion of dinosaurs hunching at the hilltops along the road, silhouetted in purple by flashes of lightning. What a night! Nothing much ever happens on the

STONEHENGE OF CLAIBORNE COUNTY. I never tire of Windsor and its shifting shadows and changing moods. No wonder it's hard to capture in photography. It is always changing.

four-lane except you can zip farther quicker than you were able to before. But there's little left to see, so why not zip on down the road?

About the only section of lower 61 that may still even remotely resemble that old description is the mile or so where (as of right now) they have yet to bypass the hamlet of Lorman. That section of the highway still passes old graveyards and rises upward to allow glimpses of the blue sky just past the oaks at the top of the bluff and then falls off into a dank, humid bottom between the hilltops. There is no Spanish moss there, however. But there is kudzu to add a little character to the trees and power poles and deserted homeplaces along the way.

I miss the Old Country Store at Lorman. The building is still there, but without all the old stuff that used to clutter it when Ernie Breithaupt was alive and ran it, it just isn't the same place.

When Ernie passed away, the things in the store were auctioned off a piece at a time. So there are several thousand people who have souvenirs of the store and the era: horse collars, boxes of thread, old dresses, high-top shoes, all sorts of things.

The first time I featured the Old Country Store on *Look Around Mississippi*, I asked Ernie why he never modernized the store. He drew a deep breath and preceded what came next with, "Well sir." And then he explained how the rural, agricultural economy in which the store came into existence and was a part of ceased to exist when mechanical farming methods came into being. For a while the store struggled. And then it came time to make a decision on the future course for the Old Country Store. And Ernie said they decided to do nothing. Leave everything as it had been since the 1800s and advertise the store as a tourist destination.

And it worked. The day I was there, I came in just as a busload of people from the Netherlands was leaving. Ernie said if he had modernized, those people would have never stopped there. And he added that I'd have never come there to put it on TV. And he was right. I passed no telling how many modern stores on my way to Lorman to see his old one.

THE OLD COUNTRY STORE at Lorman managed to stay an old country–type store for a long time. It has been a flea market and is now a restaurant since the old store closed.

One thing I miss most about the Old Country Store is the hand-dipped ice cream cones. Any time I was on that end of the road, I'd give myself a treat at the end of a good shooting day with an ice cream cone from the Old Country Store. Sometimes, I'd stop in *before* I shot and reward myself for the good job I knew I was going to do that day.

A few miles farther north up Highway 61 is Port Gibson.

Back in 1995, the station sent me to St. Petersburg, Russia, to do preview stories of the "Palaces of St. Petersburg" exhibition opening the following year in Jackson. St. Petersburg was like no place I had ever seen in my life. There were canals and old, old buildings and palaces where honest to goodness royalty had lived once upon a time ago—a fairy-tale city full of old churches and shops and theaters and cemeteries.

After a week there, I noticed the people of St. Petersburg walking past all of those places and never particularly looking up. It dawned on me that they were around all of this every day of their lives. This was just where they lived, to them. Realizing that, I decided I never would want to live anywhere I thought was magical or enchanting for fear that in seeing it every day, it would become ordinary and humdrum.

That's the way I have grown to feel about Port Gibson. It is a special little town with a dreamlike ambiance. But I know if I lived there I would end up getting involved in politics and water system issues and grow concerned about crime and unemployment. Not that those aren't admirable things to get involved with, but those sorts of things tend to knock the pixie dust off a place. And I'd rather stay enchanted with Port Gibson.

The slogan on the welcome sign says the Union Army thought a lot of the village when they marched through here on their way to Vicksburg in 1863. "Too beautiful to burn" says the sign, attributed to General U. S. Grant. Maybe he said it, maybe he didn't. But he didn't burn it.

OLD TOWN, PORT GIBSON. The date on the building attests this was one of the ones "too beautiful to burn" during the Civil War.

The town's most famous landmark is the steeple of First Presbyterian Church. On top of it is a twelve-foot-high carved hand pointing toward heaven. The gold-leaf finger can be seen from all over town. Why did the founders of the church want a heavenward hand on their steeple instead of topping it with a cross or just a pointy roof? There are two versions.

The more likely of the two suppositions says the first pastor of the church used a similar gesture from the pulpit when making points in his sermons. The other says a house of less than honorable morals used pointing hand placards nailed to trees and stuck on the sides of buildings around town to point the way to their front door. It worked for them, so the church adopted the symbol for a higher use.

There could be no more photographed steeple in Mississippi. Inside, the massive chandeliers in the sanctuary came from the steamboat *Robert E. Lee*. In the middle of each is a metal figure of the general mounted on his horse.

However, the most striking interior of any of the Port Gibson churches has to be that of St. Joseph's Catholic Church. Sunlight passing through the tall cobalt blue windows makes the whole room glow as if it were wrapped in a heavenly mist.

Elvie Bowie Moore, daughter of Jim Bowie's brother Rezin Bowie, caused her husband to be a principal benefactor of St. Joseph Church. As the church was being built, Mrs. Moore asked funds from anyone who came to the front door of their home and even went door to door seeking donations, not only from Catholics but from Protestants and even members of the Jewish community. Her husband, John Taylor Moore, finally footed the rest of the bill just to get her to stop annoying their friends.

Rezin Bowie is buried in the Catholic Cemetery just a few blocks to the east of the church. Rezin was the inventor of the Bowie knife his brother, Jim, made famous in a sandbar brawl

PORT GIBSON STEEPLE. The heavenward hand is Port Gibson's trademark, much as the Golden Gate is for San Francisco or the Empire State Building is for New York City.

COBALT BLUE windows filter sunlight into St. Joseph's Church in Port Gibson. I'd have never cut up in service like I did as a child had our church felt as hushed as these windows make St. Joseph's feel.

REZIN BOWIE GRAVE. The inventor of the famous Bowie Knife is buried here. Rezin's brother Jim, made the knife famous.

across the Mississippi River from Natchez at Vidalia, Louisiana. That knife was found on Jim Bowie's body later at the Alamo, where he was killed.

There is an unusual grave in the middle of Soldiers' Row, the Confederate section of Wintergreen Cemetery in Port Gibson. A Union soldier is buried there. Somehow he was overlooked when all the Union dead in the area were being gathered up and moved to the cemetery at the Military Park at Vicksburg after the Civil War ended. But he got a magnolia blossom beside his headstone on Decoration Day just like the boys in gray. A. K. Shaifer probably put many of those flowers there personally.

The Shaifer property was located out west of Port Gibson some several miles. April 30, 1863, was a busy day around the house. Grant's troops had crossed the Mississippi River and landed at nearby Bruinsburg that day. Near midnight that night, the women of the Shaifer house were still feverishly loading wagons, trying to get away to Port Gibson before the Union troops got there. The Shaifer men were in the Confederate Army off serving elsewhere at the time.

Confederate General M. E. Green rode up in the yard of the Shaifer house on horseback about midnight to assess the situation. His troops were deployed a mile back down the road toward Port Gibson at Magnolia Church. The general tried to assure the panicking Shaifer ladies that they could calm down. He told them that nothing was going to happen before sunup.

About that time a vanguard of the advancing Union Army engaged Confederate sharpshooters, and the first shots of the campaign for Vicksburg were fired right there in the front yard of the Shaifer house.

To this day there are still holes in the walls of the Shaifer house put there by stray minié balls fired that night.

ST. JOSEPH'S CATHOLIC CHURCH in Port Gibson glows a heavenly blue as sunlight filters through the church's cobalt blue window panes.

BRUINSBURG MARCH MARKER. This sign is way out in the wilderness on the very road Grant and the boys marched down in 1863. This is a still frame from the Grant's march video.

SOLDIERS' ROW. Another still video shot from a *Look Around* story about Memorial Day and how A. K. Shaifer used to celebrate it in Port Gibson.

Libby Shaifer Hollingsworth, a descendant of A. K. Shaifer, told me that a couple of years after the Civil War ended, Mr. Shaifer got a letter from William Duffner of Mitchell, Indiana, asking about the lay of the land around the Shaifer property. He had been a member of Grant's army marching across the Shaifer place and was evidently trying to remember the particulars of the battle.

A friendship struck up between Duffner and Shaifer. Duffner came for visits back to the Shaifer farm along with other members of the company. Reunions were held there at the Shaifer house of the men in blue who had battled across the adjoining land in 1863.

A. K. Shaifer went back to Indiana to visit Duffner and was even invited to address a meeting of the GAR, perhaps the only Rebel ever to do so.

As the former soldiers began to age, they started passing away. Every year for Memorial Day, which is what Decoration Day evolved into, Shaifer would pick boxes of fresh magnolia blossoms and ship them to Indiana to be placed on the graves of the old Union soldiers who had died, just as magnolia blooms were also being placed on the graves on Soldiers' Row in Port Gibson.

DUFFNER PAINTING. William Duffner painted what he remembered of the Port Gibson Battlefield on the seat and back of a rocking chair and presented it to his friend, A. K. Shaifer. The chair is in the Grand Gulf Park Museum.

His friends in Indiana would take photographs of the decorated graves and send them back to Shaifer every year so he could see how his magnolias looked when placed there. Over time, all of the old soldiers passed away, including Mr. Shaifer. So, long since have the shipments of magnolias to Indiana ceased. And sadly, so has the practice of decorating the graves on Soldiers' Row in Port Gibson.

My father was in World War II. He never talked about it to me with the exception of answering "no" when I asked him if he ever killed anybody. Mama said when he first got home he wanted to someday take her to the Po River Valley in Italy where he served. After a while, talk of that evaporated.

But the soldiers of the Civil War were different, maybe because the war was fought within the borders of the country and against fellow countrymen. But there seemed to be a need to talk it out and reminisce among the participants. Libby Hollingsworth says she thinks it was some sort of healing process to go and see where the battle was and see that peace had returned.

Or maybe the boys in blue were like me: they just fell in love with the bluffs and sunken roads and blind curves and the remoteness of those roads out in the western part of Claiborne County and just had to have a "fix" of them from time to time.

The most famous road that ran through the area is the Natchez Trace. Just outside Port Gibson there is a preserved stretch of the old sunken Trace. Over time, foot

SHAIFER HOUSE, PORT GIBSON BATTLEFIELD, is where the first shots were fired by the Union as they started heading inland toward Vicksburg.

PORT GIBSON EXIT. The Natchez Trace walking path was very old when these cars were new. Thank goodness it's paved now. Port Gibson is where the Trace intersects with Highway 61.

SUNKEN TRACE. A portion of the ancient walking path has been preserved near Port Gibson.

and hoof traffic and wagon wheels pounded the roadbed deep into the soft loess soil. This preserved area of the original pathway is ten or fifteen feet below the surface of the surrounding land.

I wanted to get a shot of the old Trace for a *Look Around Mississippi* story one day but needed some perspective so you could tell what you were looking at. Things that are perfectly clear in three-dimensional eyesight can become very confusing when compressed down into two-dimensional photography.

I set the camera up on the lip of the gully so Jo could follow as granddaughter, Taylor, and I walked the path on the floor of the depression. A bee flew by. Taylor is deathly afraid of anything that is small and flies and buzzes. She started flailing her arms to ward off a bee attack. The video looks like she is trying to swim.

Dogwood is one of my favorite spring flowers. I didn't realize it when I was younger, but we didn't have naturally occurring dogwood in the Delta. I didn't miss it because I had never seen it except when we would go to the hills. I knew that pines never made it down the hills into the flat Delta.

There is plenty of dogwood in the hollows between the hills in the bluffs area of the state. I associate it more with Claiborne County than any other. There are more ridge-top back roads there, maybe. Watching the world wake up after winter on those back roads is amazing.

Before anything comes into full leaf, the dogwoods appear. Dogwoods grow in the understory of the woods. They aren't big trees at all. A thirty-foot-tall one would be a giant. Due to a lack of light where they thrive best, they are usually pretty spindly, too.

In middle to late March, they start popping out in the lower part of Mississippi, and the blossoming works its way northward at the rate of about twenty-five miles a day. So by the first part of April, the valleys between the high hills out in the bluffs are dotted with white dogwood blooms as far as you can see.

And the blooming of the dogwood is a thing you'd have to see, too. It is impossible to capture it adequately in photographs. Video is a little better because you can pan the camera to get the full effect of white specks everywhere. But to pull the lens

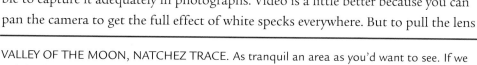

VALLEY OF THE MOON, NATCHEZ TRACE. As tranquil an area as you'd want to see. If we only had time to stop and enjoy it sometime.

CORNFIELD, CLAIBORNE COUNTY. Fall alongside the Natchez Trace either looks like this or, in alternate years, is white with cotton.

DOGWOOD AND BLUE SKY. Sure sign that spring has returned to the bluffs.

wide enough to see what the eye sees renders the blooms so small that they become almost invisible, blending in with the flecks of light reflecting off the bare bark of the emerging hardwoods around them.

And then it's over. Two weeks later, the dogwood leafs out, and the white blooms are gone. And green overtakes the world again. Spring greens are different from summer greens. In spring the trees in the bluffs are lighter and darker shades of green. Some are yellow-green at first. Each tree is an individual. You can pick them out. And here and there a wild maple is still showing its flaming red blooms as it makes its propeller seeds.

The heat returns pretty quickly in this part of the country. By the end of May, it will have already topped ninety degrees some days. And spring greens will darken and turn into a summer uniformity in no time.

Hot May temperatures remind me of when they were filming Willy Morris' *My Dog Skip* in Canton. It was May and it was a *hot* May. *Skip* was a low-budget movie, meaning they hoped to bring the whole thing home for under five million dollars.

I got a call at the TV station one afternoon from someone associated with the movie asking if I had any footage of whitetail deer. I told him no, and I don't know why, but I added that I *did* own a '46 Ford pickup. Why I associated the two, I can't remember. But the guy got all excited when he found out the truck ran. He said they had lots of "parkers" but not many "runners."

Coupled with my owning a truck the movie needed, my also knowing Jo Ann Gordon with Canton Tourism gave me a lock on show business. Next thing I knew, I was in a movie. Well, I took my truck to Canton and drove it around a lot in the background while they made a movie down at the other end of the block from me.

But it was hot. I don't know if it was unnaturally hot or if I was just out in it when I was used to being inside or in an air-conditioned car in that kind of heat.

But my '46 is not air-conditioned except for open windows and motion. And you don't move a lot making short clips of a movie. So I was glad when I got to park the truck and get out and just watch for a while.

RETURNING SPRING. Old home places are awash in flowers in the spring. You may not ever know another thing about the people who used to live there, but you can tell the kinds of flowers they liked.

One of the scenes I got to watch them film was the one where Skip drives the car. In the book, Willy Morris writes about a practical joke he used to pull as a boy on the folks in Yazoo City, where the story is set, by propping Skip up on the steering wheel while he hid below and worked the pedals and steered. And it looked like Skip was driving.

So they got ready to shoot that scene and had the actor dog propped up on the steering wheel while a movie crew grip got on the floorboard as described in the book.

This guy had more to handle than two people could do. He had to work the clutch, accelerator, brake, and steering wheel, plus operate a walkie-talkie at the same time. I guess it never occurred to anyone that Willy may have been writing fiction about being able to control a car while sitting in the floor.

Well, the director got everything in place, lights set so the dog stood out, camera mounted on a traveling dolly to pace with the car. Action! The clutch popped, and the car nearly wiped out a whole row of "parkers" while repeated shouts of "cut" reverberated off the store fronts, as if that would stop the dog-car.

But the grip kept his cool, averted the catastrophe, and modified his clutch touch, and the scene was shot again.

They managed to get enough footage of four tires rolling on the ground and a dog at the wheel to establish the fact that Skip was driving the car and finished out the rest of the episode with tight shots filmed with the car being pulled on a trailer.

Then they wanted to get one more scene shot before we broke for lunch. This time, young Willy's mother was to drive a car around a corner and yell some exciting news out the window to the kids on the street.

I don't think the actress driving the car had ever driven a standard shift. And a '36 Chevy probably isn't the best car in which to learn how to drive one. She'd snatch out the clutch and the car would stall. Or it would buck jump and jerk around the corner.

OVERLOOK, BAYOU PIERRE. West of Port Gibson. Where Bayou Pierre empties into the Mississippi River is where Bruinsburg was located.

CULTURAL CROSSROADS QUILTS are handmade and for sale at the Crossroads Building in Port Gibson. Crossroads is dedicated to racial harmony and economic improvement.

Finally, after about forty-five minutes of shooting, she got it down and smoothly released the clutch, made the left-hand turn, and delivered her line. Then we broke for lunch.

I overheard someone in the lunch tent make the comment, "Ya know, the dog drove a lot better than the lady, didn't he?"

Well, enough for the side trip; back to Port Gibson. Another of the buildings here that makes Port Gibson a mystical place is Temple Gemiluth Chassed, the oldest surviving synagogue building in Mississippi. The name means "Acts of the Righteous."

The building is unique in Mississippi architecture with its squared-off onion dome on top, just above twin key-hole-arched windows over the main entranceway. The entrance outside and the Ark inside (the recess where the Torah was stored) are of the same keyhole design. It looks like something out of *Casablanca* or *1001 Arabian Nights* or something. The style is described as Byzantine, Moorish, Romanesque on the historic marker out in front of it.

Marty Nathanson, sort of the unofficial rabbi and one of just a handful of remaining members of the Natchez synagogue, told me that Napoleon's sweep across Europe was most responsible for the Jewish settlements in Mississippi. To get away from the wars, Jewish families from the Alsace region of France and Germany got on boats headed for America. New York or New Orleans, it didn't matter to them. Look on the headstones in the Jewish cemeteries in Natchez and Port Gibson and Grand Gulf and so on, and you'll see many people buried there who were natives of that region of Europe.

Once in port, they started migrating up the Mississippi River. They settled in communities like Natchez and Fayette and Port Gibson and Vicksburg and Greenville. Most were merchants; many became cotton

ETERNAL FLAME. This light is never turned off in the old synagogue in Port Gibson. Before electricity it was a gas light.

TEMPLE GEMILUTH CHASSED is the oldest Jewish synagogue building left in the state. It's on Church Street in Port Gibson.

brokers. They stayed in the small communities until the centers of commerce started gravitating to the larger cities—New Orleans, Jackson, Memphis.

In 1891 when Gemiluth Chassed was built, the Jewish population of Port Gibson was more than one hundred people. In 1991, when they celebrated the one hundredth anniversary of the Temple, there was not a single Jewish person left living in the town. There were fewer than twenty-five Jewish individuals in Natchez then, down from more than 150 families at one time.

With the declining Jewish population in Port Gibson, the town nearly lost its landmark Temple. The fixtures had already been removed and taken to the Museum of the Southern Jewish Experience at the Henry S. Jacobs Camp in Utica. The building was scheduled to be demolished and replaced with a car wash.

One of Port Gibson's most active families, the Lums, stepped in and bought the Temple and set out on a restoration odyssey that will last as long as the family does, I suppose. They shored up the building and stabilized the structure and fixed up and painted. But there is always going to be something else that needs to be done to a building that old when you are paying for it out of your back pocket. Bill Lum told me that he was able to get the original fixtures back from the Museum.

The synagogue is a mystical-looking place where you could easily imagine flying carpets might come floating out of its windows. I love the ladder-back chairs in the front of the sanctuary. The uprights have carved birds' heads on the tops. They remind me of Mary Poppins' umbrella handle, except these chairs don't talk. However, they weren't original to the synagogue, I found out later, but belong to Martha Lum. She put them there from her house.

FIXTURE, GEMILUTH CHASSED. The original chandeliers were donated by a New Orleans family to the synagogue.

TEMPLE CHAIR DETAIL. The ends of the back uprights are carved to look like birds' heads. Just another oddity in a town where I've grown used to finding unusual things.

DOGWOOD blooms are the sure sign of spring. Always satisfied to grow in the understory of the woods, the white blossoms fill spaces until green leaves start to grow again.

FALL SPIDER LILIES are everywhere old houses used to be. Once they may have been in a neat row. But I've seen fields where acres have run wild from old home places.

ROCKY SPRINGS METHODIST CHURCH. It and its cemetery are the only survivors from a thriving community a century and a half ago.

The Greenville that I grew up in during the 1950s and '60s was a comfortable amalgam of influences from many cultures. We had a strong Jewish contingent and an equally strong Italian Catholic contingent, as well as a Chinese community, leavened among those of us of the more usual Scottish-Irish-English and African American backgrounds. It made for a grand place to be born and raised, and though I know life is made up of change, I am saddened to think that the Jewish heritage of those days may soon be only a memory.

There is magic in Port Gibson that will cast a spell on you. From hundred-year-old initials of schoolboys who slipped into the attic of the dorm at Chamberlain Hunt Academy to leave their names in chalk on the rafters, to the wind whispering around the steeples of the churches and the synagogue. From the dogwoods and azaleas of spring to the spider lilies of autumn. From the memory of the flavor of the curry-sprinkled, bacon-wrapped beef filets at the Old Depot Restaurant (now closed) to the way the cotton-seed oil mill smells and makes you hungry.

It's all exuberating when all you are doing is passing through. The antebellum homes, spooky old cemeteries with their unusual grave markers, churches with yawning sanctuaries; it's all surreal when I can just zip into town on my imaginary flying carpet and sample enough of it to do another story and then leave again before staying long enough to float to earth and get involved in issues like potholes and city ordinances.

One thing General Grant and I agree on for sure: Port Gibson is a beautiful town. I'm glad he didn't burn it. Everybody needs to have a Brigadoon, a place that time hasn't spoiled. And if I just pretend some things are invisible, Port Gibson is that place for me. A runaway I can escape to and put on blinders and see the magic. Oh, the magic is real. The blinders just shut out the everyday things that don't fit. Gasoline prices and stuff like that.

But if we stay too long, the clock will strike midnight and the coach will turn into a pumpkin and it will all disappear. So let's put Claiborne County in the rearview mirror and press on northward up Highway 61 into Warren County.

CLAIBORNE COUNTY COURTHOUSE. The building dates from the 1840s and replaced a log courthouse that burned in 1839.

MAGNOLIA BLOSSOM. Summer drifts in on the fragrance of magnolias.

THE MISSISSIPPI RIVER is always the backdrop to everything going on up on the shore and into the bluffs and inland towns. It's the personality of the whole area.

Vicksburg & Warren
COUNTY

ONE OF THE FIRST *LOOK AROUND MISSISSIPPI* STORIES I WANTED TO DO in Warren County was to find one of the handful of surviving siege caves from the Civil War and take a peek inside. I knew they existed, but I had no idea where any were. So I called the Old Courthouse Museum in Vicksburg and was connected to Gordon Cotton. At that time I didn't know Gordon, and since he didn't own a television set, Gordon didn't know me.

I told him who I was and what I wanted to do. Fine. Until I got to when I wanted to do it—the next Saturday. Out of the question, Gordon said. He explained that he hadn't had a day off in three months and had already made plans for that day. Being the self-centered individual that I am, I couldn't fathom why anyone wouldn't gladly give up his plans to spend a day doing what I wanted to do in order to help me get a story that I so desperately needed. But Gordon let me know pretty quickly.

I was deeply hurt by Gordon's candor. However, secretly I admired him because I've never been able to do that. I've gotten into more fixes and am what I am today because I have always taken the path less offensive. I'm a prime example of how you wind up when you take the course that hurts the fewest feelings, no matter how much of a bind it puts you in.

Gordon, sensing my pain, suggested I call Terry Winschel at the Vicksburg Military Park. Maybe he could help me. Later on, Gordon and I got to know each other better over other projects and since have become good friends.

THE OLD COURTHOUSE, VICKSBURG, houses one of the finest Civil War museums in the nation. Diaries of the men in the trenches tell their version of the siege.

Let me tell you a little more about Gordon before we come back to the siege caves. Over time, I have needed his expertise on several topics. I'll phone him and ask him whatever it is I need to know. His end of the conversation usually begins, "Well, I don't know much about it, but..." and then he continues for forty-five minutes to an hour as he tells me all he "doesn't" know. I've met few people as knowledgeable as Gordon.

The last story I did with Gordon was when he and his associate were having a signing for a book they had just published of excerpts from Civil War diaries from the archives at the museum. Gordon was as upbeat as usual that day. I have never seen a time when he wasn't. And as proof of that, when Vicksburg funeral director Charles Riles came in to get his copy of the book autographed, instead of things getting somber, that's when the party really began.

Gordon started telling stories about Charles. One of the adventures happened about two months earlier, around Groundhog Day. Charles had been involved with a funeral in the Delta. The deceased had been cremated, and whoever dug the hole for

OLD COURTHOUSE ATTIC. Gordon Cotton has culled the best from the rest from what's stored up here. But it would take one person more than a lifetime to sort through everything and be sure.

the burial dug it a little too deep. So as Charles was setting the urn in the grave, feeling for the bottom of it, he lost his balance and fell in.

After he finished telling us this story at the book signing, Gordon quickly asked him, "Well, when you climbed out of the hole did you see your shadow?"

Not too long ago, Gordon allowed me to take my camera into another of those places where not just everybody gets to go—the attic of the Old Courthouse. There are literal footprints of history up there where generals stood and watched war being waged during Grant's siege.

The Union gunboats down along the riverfront were lobbing shells into Vicksburg. Gunboat personnel have left diary accounts of seeing citizens coming out on the catwalk around the clock tower above the courthouse during bombardments, watching the shells being launched from the cannon on the boats and then rushing around to the other side of the clock tower to see where they landed. One sailor swore they were placing bets.

As far as the Union siege, Gordon told me that amazingly the Old Courthouse took just one hit during the bombardment, although it was the most prominent target on Vicksburg's skyline. One reason may have been that Union prisoners of war were being housed in the building. Confederate General Pemberton in Vicksburg reckoned that the Union bombardments would stay aimed away from their own troops.

The Union occupation during and after the Civil War wasn't a pretty time in Vicksburg. A friend of mine owns a tour home in the city that attests to that fact. The Bobb family were the third owners of the home known as McRaven. Lore has it that a

SITE OF INTERVIEW BETWEEN LT. GEN. U.S. GRANT U.S.A. AND LT. GEN. PEMBERTON JULY 4th 1863

THE STAIRCASE AT PEMBERTON'S HEADQUARTERS is sublime with its simple symmetry. The home stood through the war but was nearly lost in the peace before being restored.

THE SURRENDER SITE where General Pemberton handed over Vicksburg to General Grant may well be the exact spot where the United States got its second birthday. With Vicksburg gone, it was just a matter of time until the Confederacy would fall.

Natchez Trace bandit, Andrew Glass, started the house as a pioneer-era, over/under, bedroom/kitchen with a front gallery on both levels in the late 1700s.

Then sometime in the 1830s, Warren County Sheriff Howard removed the galleries and added a federal-style addition to the home Glass had started. The Howard Addition consists of a dining room downstairs and a bedroom upstairs with new galleries facing west toward the river. By the way, in that bedroom Sheriff Howard's teenage bride, Mary Elizabeth, died in childbirth.

Later, the Bobb family bought the property in the 1840s and added a Greek Revival parlor, flying wing staircase, and bedroom on the front of the Howard Addition. Bobb, being a brick merchant in Vicksburg, lavishly bricked walkways through the flower gardens around the house.

Came the Civil War and the siege and the occupation. One evening Mr. Bobb caught several drunken Union soldiers on the McRaven property. In anger he picked up a brick from a sidewalk and hurled it at the men and struck one of them. The group swore revenge as they staggered off. Bobb immediately reported the incident to the provost marshal, who shrugged the whole thing off and told Mr. Bobb to go home and not to worry. When the soldiers sobered up, they would have forgotten the whole thing.

CIVIL WAR REENACTMENTS are common events on the grounds of McRaven in Vicksburg. Here, soldiers are suiting up for a 4th of July celebration.

Only problem, the soldiers caught Mr. Bobb on his way back to the house while they were still drunk and murdered him. Mrs. Bobb put McRaven up for sale immediately after the funeral.

A Union soldier, William Murray, who had married a Vicksburg girl, bought McRaven and set about raising his family there. Two of the Murray daughters never married and lived out their entire lives in McRaven as recluses. As they grew too old to take care of the place, they allowed the grounds around McRaven to grow up to the point that people started doubting there was even a house in there among the trees and vines.

The two spinsters never added modern conveniences such as electricity and running water. Their physician did insist that they get a telephone in their old age in case of an emergency. That was the only device of a modern nature installed in McRaven while the sisters were still alive. There was no refrigeration in the house after the Vicksburg Ice Plant closed in 1949. In cold weather, legs off the antebellum chairs were burned in the fireplace for heat.

In the 1960s, one of the sisters died and the other moved to a nursing home, taking only her father's walking cane from McRaven with her. The house and its contents were sold. The Bradway family bought McRaven, restored it, and converted it into a tour home.

Extensive work had to be done to make McRaven presentable and to get the house to the point where it reflected its earlier glory. Vines growing through the windows upstairs in the Sheriff Howard bedroom had to be removed and the window panes replaced. There were trails connecting the rooms through the house outlined with piles and piles of stuff on either side. For example, workers found a stack of newspapers in the house with a 1965 edition on top and an 1865 edition on bottom. All of that and more had to be cleaned up.

AZALEAS AT McRAVEN have such vivid color they hurt your eyes. Azaleas of this type are no more native than kudzu. But they've become just as much a part of the South as kudzu has.

The walls needed restoration where there was even Civil War shell damage in some places. And the whole house then had to be painted inside and out.

Electricity and modern plumbing and heat and air were installed in a way that didn't take away from the historic fabric, and McRaven came back to life.

All three of its construction sections were furnished and finished in keeping with the period in which each was built. The rustic kitchen and pioneer bedroom from the 1790s at the rear of the house retained a pioneer look. Sheriff Howard's Federal dining room and bedroom were restored to that style. And the Bobbs' ornate Greek Revival section making up the front portion of the house was put back as good as new.

Some twenty years later, in the mid-1980s, the Bradways sold McRaven to my friend, Leyland French. Leyland's plans were to continue operating McRaven as a tour home, but in addition, he planned to live there. He was the first occupant of the house since the Murray sisters left. In the interim Bradway years, McRaven had just been a tour home, not lived in. And although quirky things had happened in the house during those years, such as lights turning on by themselves in the middle of the night, causing the Vicksburg police to get the Bradways to come check for intruders (and there never were any), Leyland says he had no idea the place was haunted when he bought it.

At first, all went well. The house was light and airy, but special little "things" would happen here and there. For instance, the piano stool in the Bobbs' parlor would not stay under the piano. Leyland and his tour guides found themselves constantly having to scoot it back after they had been out of the room for a while. Electric lights continued to turn on by themselves all the time.

One of the strangest incidents happened near the end of the first tourist season after Leyland bought the house. It was near the time to close the house for the winter months. There had been only a few visitors all day, and there was just one older couple in the house at the time. Since tourists were down to a trickle, Teresa Winschel was the only tour guide on duty that afternoon.

The tours start in the front portion of McRaven, the part of the house the Bobbs added in the late 1840s, then work back on the lower floor of the house through the 1830s Howard dining room, then outside to the 1790s kitchen, then back inside and upstairs to the 1790s "Pioneer" bedroom.

The Pioneer room is totally out of character with the rest of the house. Though the Greek Revival and Federal-style sections of McRaven are restored to much what they would have looked like when new, the Pioneer bedroom has been allowed to age pretty much untouched. Chunks of the original horsehide and buttermilk plaster are missing from the walls, dislodged by cannon fire during the Civil War.

THE PIANO STOOL at McRaven refuses to stay put. Some say vibrations from the railroad just outside the house move the stool. But how does it vibrate up onto the rug?

The tour guides used to play a little game to amuse themselves. They stopped the tourists at the bottom of the back stairs and then would go on up ahead inside the Pioneer bedroom at the top of the stairs. Then they'd turn and watch for the shocked expressions on the tourists' faces as they came in behind.

So Teresa did just that that afternoon with the couple. She left them at the bottom of the back stairs and told them to count to ten and come on up. Then she scampered inside the Pioneer room and turned and waited. But no one came. So she called for the couple to come on. But there was only silence down below in the stairwell.

Puzzled, Teresa went back out to the landing at the head of the stairs to see what had happened to them, but they weren't where she had left them. Teresa came back downstairs and checked the lower gallery outside. Then she went back through the house and finally found the couple, looking slightly confused, standing in the front parlor. Teresa thought maybe they had not understood her instructions to follow her up the back stairs.

Oh yes, they got that part. But before they could go up, another tour guide had come through, and they followed her back to the front of the house. This other guide was dressed much like Teresa—antebellum full hoop skirt only her hair was long, shoulder length, whereas Teresa's was up. And Teresa was pregnant at the time, and this girl wasn't.

THE PIONEER BEDROOM at McRaven has been left to age as it will. Tourists are usually shocked by the room until they explore it and discover its charm.

Then Teresa explained to the couple there was no other tour guide on duty that day and that they were the only three people in the house. At that the couple decided they had seen enough and cut the rest of their tour short.

Leyland tells me that the girl they described as having detoured them fits what Mary Elizabeth Howard looked like. Since then, Mary Elizabeth has manifested her presence several other times, always when least expected.

By the way, getting back to my original thought about Warren County, I did get to see one of the siege caves. When Gordon Cotton wanted to take his well-deserved day off, he referred me to historian Terry Winschel at the Vicksburg Military Park. I gave Terry a call, and he agreed to meet me that Saturday, when we chopped our way through waist-high kudzu about halfway up a hillside and found one of the caves.

It was "Y" shaped, with the stem opening into the hillside, then branching off into two rooms. There wasn't a lot of space in there. But when shells from the river and from the land were falling into the city, I imagine it was a lot better than standing in the open or staying in your house.

Terry Winschel and I have had several adventures together. He called me one day and told me he had just gotten a very exciting sketch in the mail from a Civil War researcher in Ohio. As the researcher was poring over diaries of soldiers serving with Grant during the Vicksburg campaign, he ran across a pencil sketch of a huge house that one of the men had drawn. It turned out to be Windsor. It is the only known picture of the house made while it was still standing.

SIEGE CAVE, VICKSBURG. During the bombardment in the spring of 1863, there were numerous caves like this dug away from the bomb blasts into the bluffs. There are about five still in existence today.

CONFEDERATE GRAVES rally around in the Vicksburg City Cemetery. There are only Union soldiers buried in the Military Park with the exception of about five Southerners who slipped in.

A DRAWING OF WINDSOR while it was still standing was found in the 1990s by a Civil War researcher going through a soldier's diary in Ohio. Terry Winschel with the Vicksburg Park holds a copy.

THE ILLINOIS MONUMENT in Vicksburg National Military Park is one of the most popular structures here. The echoes go on forever under the stone dome.

A STATUE OF A SOLDIER is one of the many bronze figures in the park. Vicksburg National Military Park has been nicknamed the "art park."

MOON AND HEADSTONE are both glowing the night of the Memorial Day 1999 celebration at the Military Park Cemetery in Vicksburg. This is a still video frame from the footage I shot that night.

The picture wasn't the Holy Grail, but it was like getting to see a drawing of it. Imagine, a hundred years after the fire, and long after anyone who had seen Windsor in person had died, we were getting a glimpse of what the old mansion really looked like. All other Windsor pictures had been drawn either from memory or from descriptions. And all others were inaccurate, according to the soldier's diary. Usually the artist left off the cupola.

While Terry and I stood in the parking lot of the headquarters of the Military Park, he took the copy of the sketch sent him out of its brown envelope, and we both searched for the exact emotion we should be feeling at such a time. Something short of awe but a little the other side of merely being impressed. And I was the first to publish the sketch on my next *Look Around Mississippi* segment that Friday.

I really enjoy places with natural beauty or history or lore. Terry took me to one spot in the Vicksburg Park that has a mixture of all three of these elements. Mint Springs Bayou originates back in the bluffs and grows larger and larger as more and more feeder streams empty into it and it meanders through the park. And then all of a sudden, its collected waters make a dramatic leap over a thirty-foot bluff and freefall onto fossil-laden boulders below. Then after gravity has collected it and calmed it again, Mint Springs flows on farther until out of the woods and turns into more or less just a drainage ditch and goes rather unceremoniously through a culvert under old Highway 61. Then it finally empties into the Yazoo Bypass Canal at the foot of Fort Hill somewhere near where the old sternwheeler *Sprague* was once docked.

The fossils at the waterfall are of the same type found in many places in Mississippi, mostly prehistoric seashells. You can find them embedded in the bank of Eubanks Creek on the nature trail at LeFleur's Bluff State Park in Jackson. And the same type of fossils are one of two wonders found at the Yazoo Clay Mine in north Hinds County near Pocahontas. The other wonder is that they can actually sell Yazoo clay!

So as far as the naturalness of Mint Springs goes, well, there it is. Water falling over a limestone ledge embedded with the fingerprints of life of the ages hidden deep in the woods in as picturesque a setting as anywhere you'd want to be.

As far as the history of Mint Springs is concerned, the waterfall and the creek below it were roughly the dividing line between Union and Confederate forces during the siege of Vicksburg in the Civil War. This particular stretch of real estate was often under an unofficial truce between the two armies as both sides came to opposite banks of the bayou to fill their canteens. Did they talk to each other? Maybe. Were

THE MISSOURI MONUMENT is another placed in the Vicksburg Park. All states that had soldiers participating on either side of the siege were invited to erect a monument.

THE EAGLE atop the Wisconsin monument is said to leave his perch and fly about the park at midnight. I'd be a lot more wary of the person who saw him do it than of the eagle.

they scared? I would be. Did they know one another? By the time the siege was over, they did.

The lore of the area is the most entertaining part. Mint Springs got its name from the abundant stands of mint growing along its banks. And Vicksburg is geographically the logical place where several elements could have come together: sugar from Louisiana heading northward, bourbon whiskey from Kentucky heading south, and fresh water and abundant mint from Mint Springs Bayou. Put it all together, and legend has it that this is the exact spot where that Southern staple, the mint julep, was invented. Right here.

One of the most moving displays I have ever seen was produced in the National Cemetery of the Vicksburg Military Park Memorial Day weekend of 1999. As a celebration of the end of the century and the end of the millennium, as well as the one hundredth anniversary of the Vicksburg Park, the graves of the 18,000 or so veterans buried there were lighted with small candles from dusk well into the night.

For weeks in advance, schoolchildren of Vicksburg had been half-filling white paper bags with sand. Then all day the Saturday of the event, those paper bags were set at the base of every headstone in the cemetery. Scout troops and other volunteers set candles in the bags. Then before the sun had set, the candles were lighted. After dark, more volunteers flitted from grave to grave resetting spent candles.

MINT SPRINGS BAYOU is another surprise in the Vicksburg Park. Lots of lore flows along with the waterfall here.

For hours a soft glow arose from each of the Union veterans' graves as well as from the graves of the five Confederates somehow buried here. And just over the bluffs, a similar lighting ceremony was taking place on the Confederate graves in the Vicksburg City Cemetery.

The sun dropped in the west behind a bank of clouds. Early on, the clouds were pink. Then as the sun sank lower, they turned a blazing orange, then ended up a deep purple against a pale azure background. All the while the ruddy glow from the thousands and thousands of candles grew brighter, sort of like the rising full moon starts off soft and glows brighter and brighter as the night darkens. The flickering flames made dancing patterns on each headstone.

Cars were bumper to bumper one way on the loop around the cemetery. Their occupants pressed against windows, taking in all there was to see of this unique event. The Indian mound at the south end of the cemetery and the brick pavilion atop it became a photographers' mecca. Flashes from disposable Kodaks all the way up to professional view cameras with tripod mounts and photographers with hoods over their heads, Mathew Brady–style, metered and snapped away until the sun was gone and the full moon rose.

I wished the dead buried there had been able to see. Maybe they did. What a night. What a sight. Flickering lights for as far as the eye could see. Fireflies in the distance. And animated silhouettes eclipsing candles here and there as volunteers attended to the sputtering.

All those lights that night. All those candles. All those graves. What a night!

I saw Terry Winschel that evening. He was obviously worn out from all the weeks of planning and coordinating and then all the activity that day of actually applying all the planning and making sure it all worked. I had my camera and interviewed him for my *Look Around Mississippi* story about the grave decorations. Terry gave me his usual perfect sound bites for which I have always admired him. But when

LIGHT 'EM UP was the order of the afternoon as volunteers descended on the Vicksburg Park Memorial Day Weekend and lit the 18,000 or so candles that glowed into the night.

LOOK AWAY...look away. And the young Confederate standing guard over the graves of his fallen brothers does just that in Vicksburg.

I asked him if the candle-lighting vigil might become an annual event, he just blankly looked at me, sort of blinking.

There is so much history in Warren County. Where the railroad bridge at Bovina crosses the Big Black River is about where retreating Confederates came over the river heading for the safety of Vicksburg after the Battle of Champion Hill. Grant and the boys came right behind them.

By the way, do you know how the town of Bovina got its name? According to my friend, Jim Brieger, in his book, *Hometown Mississippi*, the land in the area was settled by the Cowan family and the Bullen family. Seeing the "cow" and the "bull" in their last names, they came up with Bovina as a way of naming the place after both families in a way. Bovine-ah.

THE BIG BLACK RIVER RAILROAD BRIDGE at Bovina was about the last place where Grant could be stopped. Confederate General Pemberton chose instead to retreat to the safety of Vicksburg.

MEMORIAL DAY, 1999, was marked with thousands and thousands of candles lighted on every grave in both the Military Park and the Confederate section of Vicksburg City Cemetery.

THE INDIAN MOUND PAVILION in the National Cemetery at Vicksburg ties together the past with the prehistoric past and sets it here in the present for us.

When Jim was doing the research on his book, he spent fifteen years of his lunch hours, weekends, and vacations poring through the records at Archives and History, researching every place that has or ever had a name in Mississippi. The first editions of it were hand-typed and collated right there in the Brieger living room. I admire him for the effort. The result of it is an excellent research tool. And I don't know how he ever typed 557 pages on a typewriter without the aid of spell check!

As long as we're talking about books for a second, now that I am writing this book, I realize there could have easily been an entire book written about every county or town mentioned so far.

My stories on television run about two minutes. You can't say much in two minutes. So when I sat down at the computer to write this book, my first thought was that I would never be able to fill all those blank pages. But now I realize that I am just skipping a stone across a lake, barely hitting the high points as I hop across counties and regions.

So, realizing there are many more things I could write about in Warren County and Vicksburg than I'll ever get around to in this book, is it too early to begin thinking there will have to be a Volume Two? Shall we turn it into a series so we can get more things in?

With a promise to return in mind, let's slip off the last hill and into the Delta.

SUNSET OVER THE MISSISSIPPI AT VICKSBURG makes you glad the bluffs are on the east side of the river so you can get a view like this at night.

THE STEEPLE OF HOLY TRINITY CHURCH towers over downtown Vicksburg. There are several original Tiffany windows in the sanctuary of the church.

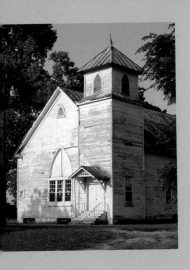

Delta
INSPIRATIONS

HIGHWAY 61 CONTINUES NORTHWARD FROM VICKSBURG and passes into another land entirely, compared with where it's been so far. That land is the fabled Delta. Physically, the Delta looks sort of like what a friend of mine said who'd never been there before. We'd driven several miles into it, and I asked him what he thought of it. After a moment of quiet reflection, he replied, "It sure is flat, ain't it?"

Another friend, Jackie Ellens, who now devotes her art almost exclusively to extracting the odd beauty of the Delta and putting it on canvas, told me after her first trip into the Delta from Jackson to attend a wedding at Hollandale that she kept looking for the pretty part.

There is beauty in the Delta. But, as Jackie discovered, you have to get to know the rest of it before the "pretty part" starts to emerge.

The Delta is flat. And there are no roads that just ease from the hills down into it. When you're driving, you sort of plunge off that last bluff as if you are diving a crop duster. And you level off not to rise again when you reach the Delta floor. And then for miles and miles and miles, you can just cruise.

The best example of a highway falling into the Delta is where old Highway 49 goes through downtown Yazoo City. The road enters town up there on the high end of Broadway and then plunges past block after block of Victorian homes that seem to be tilted into the ground on their uphill sides as your brain tries to comprehend both the steep slope of the roadway and the level lots along it. Going from the hills into the Delta is no place for bad brakes. Or ice. Gravity works well here.

ESTILL CHURCH stands ready to shepherd its flock on the banks of Deer Creek at Estill. Sunday morning religion pours as thick as Saturday night Blues over the Delta.

Driving northward on Highway 61, the Delta really begins where the road crosses over the Yazoo River at Redwood. And the highway doesn't encounter another appreciable rise until it once again climbs into the bluffs south of Memphis in Tunica County. At that spot, Highway 61 is the dividing line between the bluffs to the east and the northern end of the levee to the west. Levee Mile Marker Zero is right there beside the road.

And the attributes of the land and the people who live in the Delta, the culture they have created, the bigotry, the cotton-based aristocracy, the waves of migration, the rags to riches and riches to rags, and the people who just lived there their whole lives and never changed all that much one way or the other, these stories have filled libraries around the world and given Hollywood films and New York theaters many hours of delight. And the music emanating from the Delta inspired The Beatles and the Rolling Stones to take a whack at rock 'n' roll every bit as much as Elvis inspired them. The Delta music even inspired Elvis, for that matter.

Culturally, what's come out of the Delta is way out of proportion to its flatness. For instance, Blues music emerged by and large from the Delta. To this day, there are still pockets where the art form is authentic. But sadly, Blues has become like the sci-fi runaway computer program that became aware of itself and turned into some kind of artificial intelligence. Some might call it evolution.

But when you have people performing Blues wearing so many gold chains reflecting the spotlights from the flashing array on the metal framework overhead so brightly you can hardly look directly at them without being blinded, while their fleet of quarter-million-dollar, air-conditioned buses await them out back motors running, and the entourage on stage is complete with full brass section, multiple drummers, and redundant guitar players, not to mention traveling stage hands and a road

IN THE RAIN. The famous Blues Highway has a case of the Blues itself on rainy Delta days.

YAZOO BRIDGE. When Highway 61 hops the Yazoo River at Redwood, it descends from the bluffs into the Delta. Everything's different for the next 200 miles.

COTTON that looks this good can make a grown man cry. Bad cotton can make him cry, too. This field is near Arcola in Washington County.

manager who was born with a nasty disposition, it's hard to understand they are playing the same type music as that lone black man who wandered into the Greenville service station on Highway 82 where I worked after school and played for me one afternoon. He was walking with his guitar in one hand and his amp in the other. I guess he just needed to play for someone. Or needed to stop somewhere and rest for a minute.

He asked me if I wanted to hear something. I didn't but told him, "Sure." As a way of offering credentials as he plugged in and tuned up, he said he used to play on the radio. I don't remember what he sang. I wasn't into Blues back then. I didn't even know that was what it was called.

But he sang and played, and he thanked me for listening. I hope he didn't want money. I was young and broke and didn't know to tip anyway. But I think he just wanted someone to listen. Maybe he was cursed like the Ancient Mariner, compelled to have to sing for someone always. Last I saw him, he was walking off east down the highway. I can't remember what he looked like. But I since have come to picture him as sort of resembling what a young Son Thomas must have looked like. Thin and gaunt with the years of his life already being mapped in deep lines on his face.

I did meet Son Thomas years and years after the wandering Blues Man popped into the service station. Spent an afternoon at his house in Leland. I was very fortunate to get some video of him playing. He had developed a brain tumor that robbed him of his musical ability. Doctors at Delta Medical Center in Greenville operated on him, and his talents returned.

Mr. Thomas talked about the old days of playing Saturday night "jukes" on plantations in the Delta. And he laughed and said someone would get to shooting and

DOCKERY PLANTATION is the legendary birthplace of the art form known as the Blues. Pilgrims from around the world come here just to stand and feel the ghosts.

BAYOU ROAD, GREENVILLE, runs past a small cypress swamp. The Delta is either plowed acreage or wetland. Or a mix of the two depending on whether it's been wet or dry lately.

you'd have to duck for cover and run and couldn't come back and get your guitar until Sunday. His eyes looked way past the window in the bedroom of his shotgun house as he was telling me all of this as if he were still seeing it happening, wishing it still were those days.

I thought the funniest thing he told me was that one of his professions was working with his one-armed uncle digging graves. I could just picture someone with one arm trying to shovel a grave. Mr. Thomas said there came a drought of deaths. But his uncle assured him there were few things more certain in life than their business. Son told him that might be true, but they were going to die if someone else didn't hurry up.

'Bout that time he said they heard the whistle on the ambulance, and business was on again.

In the Delta there are Blues. Some who've never lived it perform it. Others who've never performed it live it. If you ever get the chance to hear someone who really has lived it perform it, stop and pay attention. They're getting more rare.

Literature is part and parcel of the Delta, too. We had an English teacher at Greenville High School who waxed a little too enthusiastic about her portrayal of Greenville as a town blessed with an abundance of writers. Caught up in the spirit in class one day, she told us that we could stand on any street corner in town and throw a rock, and odds are it would hit the home of a writer. The moment leaving her, coming to herself, she realized who she was talking to and quickly added, "But don't really do that."

I went to school with the children of novelists who themselves grew up to become writers. Or went to Ole Miss and became lawyers. In third grade, Mrs. Alexander pointed out that the poem *Overtones* in our English book was written by William Alexander Percy. We all knew the name because the Greenville library was

DELTA GRAYBEARDS of Spanish moss flow from cypress and oak trees in the bottomlands. You'll find Spanish moss from about Lake Beulah on southward to past New Orleans.

DELTA DAWN. The haze could be fog left over from the night or dust from fields. Either way, the effect softens the beginning of another Delta day.

named for him. We'd seen his grave near the bronze statue of his father, LeRoy Percy, in Greenville City Cemetery. Later, William Alexander's nephew, Walker Percy, would begin his writing career.

Maybe writers were everywhere in Greenville. I threw papers every afternoon for the *Delta Democrat Times* and met both Hodding Carters—Big Hodding and the III. Mr. Solomon, our junior high school principal, was the author of several children's books. David Cohn, of course, gave us two books about Delta life and the much pla-

giarized parameters of the Delta, starting on Catfish Row in Vicksburg and ending in the lobby of the Peabody Hotel in Memphis. Only now I tend to think of it as ending in the parking lot of Elvis' Graceland Mansion.

According to family legend, Shelby Foote's dog bit my sister, Ermie, when she was about eight years old as the family was walking up the sidewalk going into the library one afternoon. Ermie has no memory of the event, having spent her childhood, as she readily admits, with her nose in one book or other. She refers most questions about her childhood to sister Linda, who was actually paying attention.

Years and years later, after Shelby Foote had become everybody's favorite Civil War historian from his appearances in Ken Burns' Civil War series on PBS, I needed an expert opinion concerning a tombstone in Guntown in Lee County purporting to be the grave of John Wilkes Booth. So I called Shelby Foote. Mr. Foote didn't want to rock history in lieu of a Booth family legend and stuck with the story about John Wilkes being captured and killed in the barn in Virginia ten days after Lincoln's assassination. I thanked him and, awkward at being on the phone with a celebrity, I guess, blurted out that his dog bit my sister when he was still living in Greenville.

Since I hadn't put my statement in the form of a question, Mr. Foote didn't really know what response I was hoping for. Neither did I after I said it. So he simply graciously replied in his drawn-out, deep Southern drawl, "Tell her I'm mighty sorry." Only that's not how it sounded. There needs to be another letter in the Southern alphabet. A short "R." It would almost be pronounced like a whole "R" but would stop just this side of it but just the other side of "ah." If we had that, you'd hear better what he said. "Tell huh ah'm mahty sahrih."

THE LeROY PERCY GRAVE in Greenville can talk to you, according to someone who used to live there. Put your hands on his and ask him what he's doing there. Listen closely and he'll say absolutely nothing.

If we had that short "R," we could better spell Southern words. Like the word "water." Spell it so it spills over the tongue in all of its Southern genteelness. All three syllables. WAH-wa-tah. The dialect flows just like liquid words when spoken correctly. And it's a dying language. Few speak it anymore now that Eudora Welty is gone. We've all been linguistically homogenized by television.

Anyway, when I passed along Mr. Foote's gracious apology to Ermie, she laughed and said no apology was wanted or needed; being bit by his dog was still her only claim to fame.

The Delta is a natural incubator for artists of various types. It's the flatness. After a while, the eye sees it differently. I read about an experiment where someone was fitted with an eye device that made everything look upside down. It was awkward at first, but soon the brain was able to take the information given it and make it look normal.

Same with the Delta. Someone from the Appalachians coming to the Delta would see only flatness, compared with their mountains. They wouldn't even stumble over something so slight as the levee. But the Deltan's brain has grown to take that flatness and make it more flat in places and less flat in others, enabling one to see rises and falls and changes in height where others don't.

And this ability to exaggerate dimensions geographically translates over into life, too. I read the account of a Delta writer who entered a writing competition. The entrants were all given the same secret topic and allowed a certain length of time to finish their treatment of the subject.

To the delight of the Delta writer, the topic, when revealed, was, "The Greatest Hill I Have Ever Known." Where others, Appalachian writers, for example, might

DELTA HOME. Over the course of the thirty or so years I've passed this house, I've seen it sometimes deserted, sometimes painted and lived in. I don't know if its occupants are on their way up or down when they move in.

expound on the difficulties of tourists hiking to the top of Clingman's Dome or the beauty of Grandfather Mountain, the Deltan wrote about—what else—the levee!

He won the competition by telling of a mound of dirt 40 feet high by 200 miles long that is at once protector if it holds and tyrant if it doesn't. And how it holds people in their place inside it as much as it holds water in its place outside. He wrote of the 1927 flood and lanterns on the levee and on and on and on. About how this little hill is Big Government at work and little people doing the job.

To anyone else, the levee is a hump of dirt. But to the Delta mind trained to see more of the more and less of the less, just dirt is the last thing the levee is. Personally, if I'd been given the assignment, I'd probably have written about the Indian mounds. But that's just me.

So maybe that's why there are so many writers from the Delta. They have the ability to take the sameness of everyday life and apply to it the optical trick learned by the Deltan's eye to exaggerate the flatness, making the high points higher and the low points lower, points most other people would never see and just pass over. And as someone once said, it's the little things in life that count. And it's the little things in life, observed and defined and resolved, that make good novels. And Delta writers can pick out little things because they stand out from the everyday flatness that surrounds them. Just pitch a rock at any house in Greenville and ask whoever comes out to see what you are doing if they don't agree. (But don't really do that.)

Into the Delta from Vicksburg, the first county you come into is Issaquena. It used to have the distinction of being the only county in the state without an incorporated municipality in it. Mayersville spoiled the record not too long ago by incorporating into a township. And by the way, it's pronounced Myersville, not Mayors-ville like out-of-state TV weathercasters new to the area call it. Once.

DELTA CROSSES. This arrangement of power poles reminded me of the three crosses display you see so many places across the country. Delta summer is going on. White-hot sky and green, green fields.

CROSSROADS. A shortcut to fame and fortune awaits the person willing to sell his soul to the devil at a crossroads. Robert Johnson made doing the deed famous. It happens every day at the crossroads of life. This crossroads is on Dockery Plantation.

Several years ago, I got a call from the NBC network affiliate's news service, asking for a story from Mississippi on the occasion of Martin Luther King's birthday. I went to Mayersville and talked to Mayor Unita Blackwell. Ms. Blackwell was heavily involved in the civil rights movement and knew Dr. King fairly well. As we walked the streets of her town, she pointed out street signs and paved roads and the water tower. Those were just some of the improvements under her administration.

She said just thirty years earlier she had been shot at in the streets of Mayersville. Now she was mayor. And seemingly she was loved by pretty much all of the town's citizens, black and white. You can erect as many statues to civil rights leaders as you want to, but if you really want to see a monument to the movement, come drive a paved street in Mayersville.

One of the first unincorporated burgs in Issaquena County you come to driving from the south on Highway 61 is Valley Park. It came into being as a service community on the railroad. Many towns originated to serve the same function.

C. B. "Buddy" Newman was born in a section foreman's house at Valley Park. He went on to become, among other things, Speaker of the Mississippi House of Representatives. Under the Mississippi Constitution, the Speaker of the House has as much if not more power than the Governor. And the Speaker has no term limits as the Governor does. So one could become a little emperor if he could put together enough time and supporters.

WINTERVILLE MOUNDS. Near Greenville, these hills were our playground until the state turned them into a park and made climbing them off limits.

DEER CREEK was the prehistoric Highway 61 through the west Delta. Some of the best early Native American sites in the Delta are along Deer Creek. People still live on its banks.

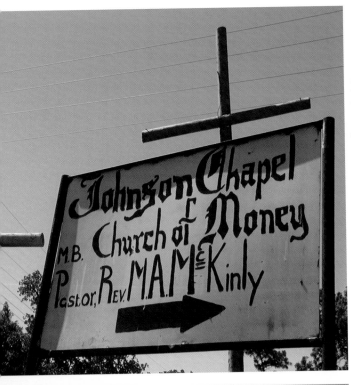

Buddy Newman did so. But as hard as he was in the halls of the Capitol, after he felt the "winds of change blowing in Mississippi," as he put it, and retired, he was just as soft back home at Valley Park.

I found him to be almost a Teddy bear of a man, putting together a railroad museum in an old boxcar on a section of Illinois Central main line he purchased and saved from being uprooted running past his back yard. The section foreman's house where he was born was restored and sat just across those tracks.

Wesley Bobo, a free spirit junk fabricator and artist from just up the road at Egremont, built Buddy a miniature locomotive to run up and down his mile of rescued railroad track. And Buddy ran the line all the time. He took me for a ride the first time I went to Valley Park when I did a *Look Around Mississippi* story about his railroad. The way he put it was that he and, "All the OTHER children of the community" liked to ride his train.

Speaking of Wesley Bobo, he's one of those people who can see useful things in a pile of junk where most folks like me would just see a pile of junk. (Ms. Jo says I'd never see the junk. I'd just step over it and keep going.) Wesley was one of the first subjects of the *Look Around Mississippi* series.

Wesley's most famous creations still adorn the bend in the road at Egremont: three dinosaurs fabricated out of spring steel blades salvaged from a cotton gin. Wesley left one rib unattached at the bottom in case someone came by and wanted to put a child inside and take a picture.

The path out to his work shed behind his house was lined about waist-high with all sorts of metal the day I did the story. Old exhaust pipes, dead motorcycles, window air conditioner units, axles, brake drums, chains, and pretty much anything else. That was where Wesley gathered his raw materials and his inspiration for his next creation.

CHURCH OF MONEY. A friend riding with me when we passed this sign demanded I stop and let her get a photo of it. "At last," she said. "Someone will admit it!"

DELTA GONE. Sharecropper shacks' roofs flap in the breeze as mechanization blew in a new day for Delta laborers. One man on a tractor can do the work a hundred used to do with mules.

ROBERT L. JOHNSON
MAY 8, 1911 ~ AUGUST 16, 1938
-musician & composer-
he influenced millions beyond his time

Jesus of Nazareth, King of Jerusalem.
I know that my Redeemer liveth and that
He will call me from the Grave.
-HANDWRITTEN BY ROBERT JOHNSON, SHORTLY BEFORE HIS DEATH AND PRESERVED
AMONG FAMILY PAPERS BY HIS SISTER, CARRIE H. THOMPSON

ROBERT JOHNSON
MAY 8, 1911
AUG 16, 1938
RESTING IN THE BLUES

ROBERT JOHNSON
"KING OF THE
DELTA BLUES SINGERS"
HIS MUSIC STRUCK A CHORD
THAT CONTINUES TO RESONATE.
HIS BLUES ADDRESSED
GENERATIONS HE WOULD NEVER
KNOW AND MADE POETRY OF
ITS VISIONS AND FEARS.

ROBERT JOHNSON GRAVE. (Top) This one is at Little Zion Church on Money Road north of Greenwood and is most likely where the influential Blues Man is really buried.

ROBERT JOHNSON GRAVE. (Middle) This one is in a Johnson family plot in the cemetery behind Payne Chapel at Quito. There is little danger Robert Johnson is really buried here. But offerings at the headstone mean someone is covering all the bases.

ROBERT JOHNSON GRAVE. (Right) This one is at Mt. Zion Church at Sheppardtown on Highway 7 in Leflore County south of Itta Bena. Robert Johnson's death certificate simply said he was buried at Zion Church. For years no one knew which one.

And Wesley has the patience to keep working with it until reality is erased and whatever he saw in his mind emerges. And he does everything in his head. He doesn't sketch his projects out on paper first.

He said his wife and cousin brought a bulldozer to the house and dug a hole and buried all of his stuff in an effort to clean up the yard one time. He said it took him nearly six weeks to dig it all up again.

I asked him if he ever threw anything away. He admitted now and again he'd carry a load to the dump. "But," Wesley laughed, "I usually bring back as much as I take."

Let me tell you one more story before we leave the Delta. And it has a moral that will carry you far in life if you pay attention.

Somehow, we had picked the coldest day of the winter to come to Arcola to do a *Mississippi Roads* segment. Usually, we first shoot all of my "stand-ups," the lines I have to say on camera to move the show from one story to the next. Then the crew shoots any "B-roll," or cover shots, they need. And then we go home.

We had just had an arctic cold front come through the night before, and the wind was still howling out of the north behind it. The sky was cloudless and cold.

DELTA DOG. Near Arcola. We were asking each other, "What are you doing here?"

ST. JOHN'S CHURCH RUIN, GLEN ALLAN. Jo and I were ambling toward Hot Springs, Arkansas, after work one night. We got to Glen Allan just as the moon was rising.

ST. JOHN'S, GLEN ALLAN. This Episcopal church was established by the first Delta settlers on Lake Washington. The Civil War robbed the stained glass windows of their lead. Then an early 20th-century tornado finished off the building.

The thermometer in the ETV van hadn't registered above thirty-two degrees all morning on the way to Arcola. And with the gusty winds, the chill factor was very un-Mississippi-ish.

By the time we finished shooting my stand-ups, all my frozen lips could pronounce were vowels. So after I delivered my last line, I dedicated myself to making sure the van heater didn't go off while the crew mopped up the B-roll.

One shot our executive producer, Francis Rullan, wanted to get was some video of the oldest tombstones in the Arcola Cemetery. So the van pulled into the driveway of a home right beside the cemetery, and the crew got out. I quickly closed the door behind them to shut out the north wind that was robbing me of my heat.

At the edge of the yard between the van and the cemetery was an electric fence. Since the fence wasn't so high it couldn't be stepped over, the crew proceeded. About the time they all got across and photographer Scooter Watley was just about to set up the camera, four bulls came from nowhere and surrounded them.

The crew—Key Ivy, the producer; Francis; Scooter; and the local guy who guided us to the cemetery in the first place—immediately went back to back as if they were circling the wagons Old-West style. Scooter was holding the tripod like it was a baseball bat.

One of the bulls "marked his spot." Later, Francis said he nearly marked his, too, in the same manner.

Reluctantly, I got out of the van, careful to stay on my side of the fence, and shouted and waved on down away from the crew to distract the bulls' attention. To the credit of the crew, they got their shot of the tombstones before scampering back over the fence.

There was a long, silent, contemplative moment after the equipment was packed and we started back down Highway 61 toward home. 'Long about Hollandale, Francis finally broke the silence. "Ya know," he started slowly, "next time I come up on an electric fence, before I just automatically go across it, I think I'll just stop and ask myself, 'Now why do you suppose this thing is here?'"

Words of wisdom. I use them every day in some sense or another.

Let's press on to the prize!

"DARKNESS ON THE DELTA" was the name of WJPR's nighttime easy listening program. Joel Netherland, the host, almost whispered the segues between the songs. I still think the Delta can get that still after the sun sets.

DELTA DUSK. Some parts of the Delta look uninhabitable. Then you see the power poles.

Getting Back
ON THE ROAD AGAIN

WE'RE NOT QUITE THROUGH YET. However, this is the last chapter, and there's so much yet to see and say that I'm not quite sure where to start. I heard a fellow stand up to give a speech who opened his remarks by saying that he didn't know where to start. And someone in the back of the room blurted out, "Start toward the end."

Yet here we are near the end, and I feel like we've hardly started. There's the whole eastern side of the state we haven't talked about yet, as well as lots of the central parts. Plus, I've yet to mention landmarks along the Gulf Coast like the Biloxi Lighthouse. It was painted black for a while after Lincoln's assassination.

Blanche Terry, who was the longtime manager of the Old Courthouse Museum in Vicksburg, told me a story that her father used to tell about another presidential encounter in Mississippi.

Blanche said her father was a teacher, and he had long since discovered that if you couple a story to whatever lesson you're trying to teach, it helps students learn better and retain the knowledge longer.

Blanche said one of her father's favorite stories concerned Teddy Roosevelt's 1902 bear hunt. It was common knowledge that Holt Collier of Greenville, former slave, former Confederate soldier, former cowboy, had the best bear dogs in Mississippi. Roosevelt was coming to the Delta to hunt bear, so Mr. Collier was approached by organizers of the hunt on the availability of his dogs. Holt Collier replied that he didn't rent his dogs to anyone.

THE BILOXI LIGHTHOUSE is one of the landmarks we need to revisit sometime. The lighthouse has survived every hurricane including Katrina since it was built. It was painted black for awhile after the death of President Lincoln.

The men were incredulous and reminded him, "But Mr. Collier, this is the president!" To which Holt replied, "I don't care if it's Booker T. Washington. I don't rent out my dogs."

Well, if you know the rest of the story, then you know Holt Collier wound up being the guide for the party and, after a fruitless day's hunting on the part of the president, Holt lassoed a bear on a bet.

Some quick-thinking aide suggested they tie the animal and let the president come shoot it. But Roosevelt was too much of a sportsman to shoot a tethered bear, and the cub was released.

Clifford Berryman, a cartoonist with the *Washington Post*, sketched the incident, and it was published in the paper. In the cartoon, Roosevelt's back is turned away from a cow-eyed cub over the caption, "Drawing the line in Mississippi."

A toy maker in New York saw the cartoon and contacted Roosevelt to obtain permission to use the president's name in association with a line of stuffed bears he intended to market under the name of "Teddy Bear."

Had it not been for Roosevelt's bear hunt in Mississippi in 1902 and Holt Collier with his lasso, we would have never had our favorite snuggly toy when we were wee ones.

Gosh, I feel bad that I didn't get us any farther than we got on this trip. We covered a pretty good bit of territory but not nearly as much as I had hoped to cover. We never made it to Tishomingo State Park way up northeast, for instance, another of my favorite hideouts.

We didn't get the chance to go to the Neshoba County Fair in this book, either. Life gets loose at the fair. People

HOLT COLLIER of Greenville was given this Confederate headstone in 2004 in honor of his service to the South during the Civil War. He's buried within a mile or so of where he killed his first Delta bear when he was around ten years old.

DON'T START NUTHIN'. Cabins at the Neshoba County Fair are busy places with people coming and going in and out as they please. I've asked many people how the fair has changed over the years. EVERY one of them starts off by saying, "Well, we have flushing toilets now."

leave the real world behind and come to the fairgrounds and reacquaint themselves with their cabin neighbors whom they get to see just this one week of the year.

One fair resident told me you become "fair related" during that week. Bonding. It's the stuff countless movies have been based on. Strangers on Monday, solving each other's problems by Saturday. (Or becoming each other's problems by Saturday!)

People pass from cabin to cabin, and total strangers act as if they have known each other all their lives, at the Neshoba County Fair. And some folks get a little goofy. One fellow told me of an instance when a guy wearing jumper cables for a belt came up on his cabin porch and asked if he could go in and get a drink of water. "Sure." "But," the cabin owner added as the stranger was opening the screen door, "don't start anything while you're in there." (Jumper cables. Don't start anything. Get it?)

Gotta mention Elvis. Back when I was doing the *Millennial Moments* series in 1999, I knew I wanted to do a story about Elvis and his Tupelo roots. But I didn't know exactly what to do. I couldn't shoot inside the birthplace house. I couldn't even use any Elvis songs or any photos of Elvis or footage without first getting permission from the Presley estate at Graceland. And I hardly had time to go shoot, much less wait around for permission forms to be filled out and approved.

THE OLD SETTLERS CABIN at Tishomingo State Park at once makes you wish you'd lived in much simpler times and also makes you glad you didn't, with no electricity or running water or mosquito screens. Too bad we have to make our own times too complicated to enjoy, sometimes.

THE ROCKS AT TISHOMINGO STATE PARK can transport you away from the topography typically associated with Mississippi. Had I grown up there, I'd have climbed them. Now I just take pictures of them.

So I just took off for Tupelo one day in hopes I'd come up with something. I got a shot of the exterior of the house where Elvis was born. Anything you can see from a public street is legal to put on TV. And I even found the family plot in the cemetery where Elvis' twin brother, who died at birth, is buried. Unmarked grave, of course. And the only other thing I could think of to shoot was Tupelo Hardware, where Elvis bought his first guitar.

So I zipped downtown and started to pull out my camera and just grab some video of the store front and go home. Then I'd take all of these elements and put something together.

Now, if I had been on my home turf, I'd have just shot the store front and left. But being in Tupelo, I decided to at least let the folks in the store know who I was and what I was up to. So I went in and met the nicest people you could ever want to meet. And the man welcoming me said it would be perfectly all right to get some shots of the store. They had people in there all the time wanting to do so. Just the week before, the BBC had been there and shot two days.

He told me the hardware store office was elevated and open in the middle of the store, and I could get some great shots of the whole inside of the place from up there. I really just wanted an exterior shot, but he was being so nice, and I didn't want to mess it up for the next guy wanting footage, so I climbed the stairs and set up my camera and hosed down the inside of the store with my lens and thanked him and started to leave.

TUPELO HARDWARE is where the culture of the Western world (actually all the world, now) started changing when Elvis Presley got a guitar here. You can still buy guitars at Tupelo Hardware today.

As he was walking me toward the door, he stopped in front of a glass display case and told me that this was the very case where Elvis bought that guitar and that people from all over the world had come in just to touch it. The glass on top was well frosted from being rubbed.

I looked at the case and I looked at my camera. All I wanted was a pan shot of the front of the store. But here was the case and here I was. So why not? I snapped the camera back onto the tripod and powered it up. I panned the case and even got a tight shot of a photo of Elvis displayed in it, thinking I could get away with showing this photo on the air since it was in the context of a display case and not necessarily just a photo of Elvis.

I thanked my host again and started to leave. About that time, a gray-haired gentleman walked in the back door, and the fellow accompanying me jabbed me on the shoulder and pointed and said, "Now that's the guy you want to talk to. He was here the day Elvis bought his first guitar" and nodded his head in the direction of the man who was already headed our way.

Well, they were being so nice, and I really wasn't in that big a hurry. A couple more minutes wouldn't hurt, and then I could get the shot I originally came to get and head out.

The man coming in the back was Bill Booth. His daddy had started the store. Bill is the owner now. The salesman on duty the day Elvis got the guitar was Forrest Bobo. Since all I had wanted was a shot of the front of the store, when Bill came up I really couldn't even think of a question to ask him. So I just made some inane comment like, "So this is where Elvis got his first guitar, huh?"

"Yes," Mr. Booth started slow, "but most folks don't know he didn't come in here for a guitar." Well, I didn't know that. Maybe all of a sudden I was glad I hadn't been in any big hurry. Maybe I was going to get a story after all.

"He was ten or eleven years old and wanted a .22 rifle. He had been stopping by the store for a few weeks after school eyeing it. And one day he brought his mama in

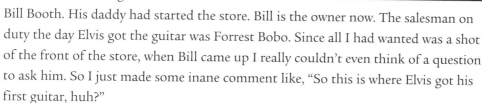

ELVIS BIRTHPLACE, TUPELO. I've not seen a survey, but I'd imagine this is one of the most visited places in Mississippi. If Elvis could start here and end up in Graceland, so could I. As a matter of fact, I have visited Graceland!

147

to get it for him. She found out what he wanted and told him flat-out no. He was too young for a rifle. So Elvis threw a fit. And to calm him down, a salesman pulled a guitar out from behind the counter and offered it to him instead. But no, Elvis wanted that gun.

"His mama told him he was going to get the seat of his pants dusted for acting like that out in public. And it was the guitar or nothing. So Elvis reluctantly took the guitar.

"And Mrs. Presley told him on the way out, 'Who knows? If you get good at that thing, you might get famous!'"

And Elvis Presley changed everything. About the time his songs started coming out, "little records," 45 rpm's, were taking over. And phonograph companies started making small personal record players that kids took to their rooms to listen to their own music choices by themselves. Until then, by necessity, children had listened to pretty much whatever music their parents had listened to.

But just when a personality came along to pied-piper the younger generation away from the older, technology and everything else fell into place to accommodate it. And a cultural shift was started that hasn't stopped since. Literally, the world hasn't been the same since the day Elvis got a guitar instead of a .22 rifle at Tupelo Hardware Store on Main Street in Tupelo.

Well, enough rambling.

It's funny how life can give you just what you want if you'll let it, isn't it? Elvis got his guitar even though at the time he had no idea that's what he wanted. Me? I would have no other job in the world than this one. If I could write out my job description, it would be exactly what I've been assigned to do. (Well, a little more pay. But that's everybody.) Yet, looking back, I was pushed kicking and screaming into it. I always thought I'd live out the rest of my life as the next Woodie, doing weather. Instead, I get to be the first Walt and explore our state and meet its people and unwrap the layers it's all bound up in.

And I think it took sitting down for the past few months and writing out some of my adventures to remind me how much I love this job. I always knew it, but it's like loving your wife. You just need to look at her sometime and realize how special she really is.

NETWORKING. It's funny how it all connects. Here I've talked to the man who sold Elvis a guitar. And I talked to a man in Yazoo City who talked to an elderly woman who was in Ford's Theatre the night Lincoln was shot. Just a couple of degrees away from two of the most momentous occasions in American history and culture.

I have one last story I want to get in before we call it quits. I debated whether to use this story or not. But I end up telling it just about everywhere I go. And when my friends found out I was writing this book of adventures out on the road, they all just assumed this incident would be in here. (Now I'm afraid I'm building it up too much, and you'll be disappointed at the outcome.)

But the incident made fast friends of Ron Evans and me.

Ron works at ETV and went with us as our audio engineer the first couple of seasons of *Mississippi Roads*. We always did at least two episodes of *Roads* every time we went out, usually one segment on Saturday and another on Sunday.

This particular Saturday we were in the Delta and had just finished with whatever show we were doing and were traveling south on Highway 1 toward Greenville, where we would be staying the night.

The next day we were going to do an entire show featuring the Mississippi River. I had written more of that show than any other *Roads* show I had been involved with up until then. And as we were going through Rosedale, I had the bright idea that we could get a jump on the next day's shooting by stopping at the Great River Road State Park, walking out to the Mississippi River, and using the late-day sun to our advantage to get some of the stand-ups in the can early.

No one objected, especially Ron, because this was his last trip out with us. The next Monday, Ron was to start a desk job. And he sensed that whatever we shot today, we wouldn't have to shoot tomorrow, and he would get home earlier on this, his last shoot with *Mississippi Roads*. Besides, it was still fairly early, and none of us were in any particular hurry to get to the hotel. Fine. We'd do it.

Key Ivy was driving and pulled into the parking lot. As the crew was unloading the gear, I walked over to the river bank to get an idea of where the water was. The last time I was shooting a story at the park, the river had been high, and water came all the way up to where I was now standing.

LUCKY DOG SHOT. Had the sun and clouds and light not been just right and the Mississippi River show won some awards, I still might have been just a nameless motel room statistic. Nice to be in the right place at the right time. And then look up and realize it.

DUCKS know it's easier to walk on the water than on the sandbar. We did shoot lots of footage of the Mississippi River that day. Next time we need pictures, I'm sure we'll go to the file tape closet and not back to Rosedale.

LANDMARK, LUCEDALE. The Coca-Cola sign comes off the old barn when hurricanes threaten. If it's not put back right away, the owner starts getting phone calls from neighbors. It's the little things that help us keep track of life.

SAND DOLLAR FOSSILS from the Chickasawhay River prove this area was once under sea water. I find fossils like this or the snails imbedded in the loess bluffs or the whale bones in Yazoo County to be an endless source of fascination.

FIRST CLASS. I stop and snap mailboxes every now and then. It's nice to run up on one that makes you laugh. Or one that just looks different from all the rest of them.

ROUND BARN. We were driving along through Tippah County just ambling our way toward Ripley to shoot a couple of stories for *Mississipppi Roads* and *Look Around Mississippi* when we saw these barns. The scenery is there for the looking.

That day, however, after a prolonged drought, there was nothing but sandbar for as far as I could see. But there was a drop-off about a quarter of a mile out, and I assumed that the river was just beyond it.

So Key grabbed the camera, and photographer John Langford grabbed the duffle bag with its assorted extra tapes, hot batteries, and microphones. Ron got the tripod, and I just took the script and read over my lines as we walked.

If you've ever tried to walk on sand, you know how difficult it is. Every step you take makes a little hole as you break through the crust. So the first thing you have to do to make another step is climb out of the hole you just made. Then you step again and make another. So we tramped out across the quarter mile of sand, stumbling around making and climbing out of sand traps as we went. In general, we had to exert the effort normally put into about two and a half steps on concrete just to make one step in the sand.

So we were already tiring when we reached the drop-off. But instead of water being at the bottom, there was just more sand. About three or four times as much as we had just crossed. Key said it was my call. I had reasons of my own to want to get home early the next day, so I decided we should go for it.

So off we trudged across the Mississippi Desert to try to find the river.

The sand on the lower bar was no easier to walk on. I was getting winded, and I wasn't even carrying any of the equipment. We were less than halfway from the drop-off to the river when I realized this was a mistake. But, I reasoned, the river is low, so we'd likely have this kind of walk wherever we went. And we'd invested this much time and energy into it. Why turn back and waste what we'd put in so far? On we went.

NEW WAYS of doing things are symbolized by this farmer's mailbox.

OLD WAYS are acknowledged by this mailbox post.

SECURITY. I heard a radio preacher talking about growing up on a farm. They had to store corn so they could feed the mules all winter so the mules would be healthy enough to plow the next spring so they could plant more corn. He said it seemed like all they were doing was raising mules.

Dying men lose track of time, so I have no idea how long it really took us to stagger across the sandbar to the river: at least a half hour, if not forty-five minutes. And I noticed Ron kept falling farther and farther behind. And I tried not to think about him, knowing this was his last time out. And by now I'm sure he was wishing his promotion had come one shoot earlier.

But after a while, just as we had all suspected, there was water after all, and we made it to the river.

Key passed the camera along to John, who connected microphones and put in fresh tape and batteries and waited for Ron to get there with the tripod so he could set up and shoot.

In a few minutes, Ron dragged up huffing and puffing and red in the face. I thought he was just exhausted until he spoke. But as Ron slammed the tripod into the sand, I realized his problem wasn't that he was about to implode from the walk, but that he was about to explode because of it. And he did.

"I have two words for you!" Ron yelled loud enough for everybody on either bank of the river to hear, especially me. "File ——ing footage!"

Nobody corrected him and told him that was actually three words.

John put the camera on the tripod after he picked it up and dusted off the sand. And as I turned on my wireless microphone, Key gingerly asked Ron if my audio level was okay.

"It's fine!" roared Ron, not even looking at the audio meters. "Knight and Dave can fix it in post audio."

Fortunately for me, we got some wonderful video in the golden light of late afternoon, dappled as it filtered

WATER VALLEY WATERMELON is passed out free to motorists during the town's annual Watermelon Carnival. There's everything from nightly concerts to lawn mower races during the celebration.

AISLE OF HONOR, KOSCIUSKO. The flags presented to the family at the passing of a veteran are hoisted on flagpoles in the cemetery every Veterans' Day in Kosciusko. The ones who've passed on are remembered as their colors march on the breeze.

THE CANTON FLEA MARKET is one of the long-established festivals and traditions we have here. Twice a year the Madison County seat shuts down regular business for a day outdoors.

through the yellow willows on the far shore of the river. And a tugboat with a load of barges came by just as we were shooting the close and tooted its horn right on cue as if it had a copy of the script.

Then, after all the B-roll was shot and all the lines were delivered, we four packed up our belongings and turned toward the van, and all four of us stopped short in our tracks at the same time. Spirits sinking, we stood side by side motionless for a moment as the reality of having to trek back across the monster sandbar soaked in on us. I think we had all known all along we'd have to walk back the way we had come but had blocked out the thought while we were busy with shooting the script. Now crossing the bar was front and center on everybody's mind.

I knew if any of the other three of them had any energy left, they would have choked me on the spot. And I couldn't have run.

I'm sure I'd be a dead man if it weren't for the fact they would have had to have drug my limp body back across the sand. And the trip was going to be hard enough already. That thought of having to carry my body out saved my life, because the idea of merely having to serve time for my murder at that point wasn't a deterrent. Besides, any sensible judge would have let them off with suspended sentences under the circumstances.

VOTING HOUSE. People of the community pitched in and built this place in which to vote several years ago in rural Attala County. Most of the people who did the work are gone. But they left a legacy and are all remembered fondly every cold, rainy November Election Day.

PREVAILING WESTERLIES blow through the Delta and have the opposite effect on power poles from the effect the prevailing southerlies have on the live oaks on the coast. The coast oaks lean into the wind. The Delta poles flow with it.

AS IN "THE GRIM." Why someone would want a sickle engraved on his tombstone is beyond me. Unless he is saying that we're next! Ripe for the Grim Reaper's harvest! I've seen several versions of a poem on tombstones around the state:
Pause, stranger, as you pass by./ As you are now, so once was I.
As I am now, soon you will be./ Prepare for death and follow me.
On the Internet I read where someone in Texas had carved a couple more lines to this poem on a headstone there: *To follow you I'm not content./ Until I know which way you went!*

Hours later, it seemed, we made it back to the parking lot. The sun was almost gone, and mosquitoes were feasting on us, as if we weren't in enough misery already.

The crew loaded up the equipment, and we all piled in and took our respective places. Key drove, John riding shotgun up front with him. I slid across the back seat to the doorless side of the van, and Ron pointedly put the duffle bag on the seat between us as he sat by the passenger rear side door.

And a few miles down the road, I think it was probably Ron from his vantage point by the window who was first to spot the huge sign for the Port of Rosedale at the next turn. As we passed, we saw boats tied up right there just the other side of the parking lot. Had we only driven a few more miles and not stopped at the park, we could have shot the whole show and never even had to have stepped on any sand at all.

Ron turned to me and said, "You had better make sure your door is locked tonight." It was.

Fortunately, the Mississippi River show won some awards, which makes the caravan across the sands more a badge of honor now. "You ought to see what we had to go through to get those shots...." is sort of the way the conversation starts now, each of us slapping the others on the back at how smart we were to do so. I'm not even sure it was still my idea for us to walk the sandbar anymore. I think someone else has taken credit for it.

But whoever, they better keep their door locked.

Well, the spring sun is calling me away from the keyboard and back to the camera and the road. I can feel we are getting pretty close to the end of this trip. And I need to charge the batteries, get Ms. Jo to pack the snacks, and let's be off again discovering more of Mississippi.

Just looking over the daily planner, I see Dillard Eubanks is taking us out for a couple of nights on the Pascagoula River next weekend. I've heard of several more haunted houses that need checking out.

I'll be back out on the road tomorrow with my video and still cameras with me. Shooting and snapping. And I'll be hearing all sorts of stories as I go. And I'll come back home and start collecting them into the word processor and, who knows, maybe I'll pick up right here soon where we left off.

So, hopefully this will be just the first collection of photos and stories and adventures we get to put together as we continue looking around Mississippi.

THE SANDS OF TIME have shifted to the bottom for this old Delta church. We were looking for the place where the levee was breached at Mound Landing in 1927 when we saw this vine-, weed-, and tree-covered building tucked away on the bank of a bayou.

About

THE AUTHOR

WALT GRAYSON IS A NATIVE MISSISSIPPIAN. He was born and raised in Greenville, in the heart of the fabled Mississippi Delta. Walt has written and hosted the *Look Around Mississippi* series at WLBT-TV in Jackson since 1990. In addition, Walt is also the host of Mississippi Public Broadcasting's award-winning *Mississippi Roads* series.

Walt spends most of his time on the road with his wife, Jo, finding and shooting more stories about Mississippi. Walt is his own videographer and editor. All of the photographs in this book were taken by him.

"I've never tried to analyze the culture of my state all that much," says Walt. "You quit living it when you do that. That's sort of like going to medical school to learn about women. You can get a lot of good information that way, but you miss some very important things."

In this book, we discover Mississippi through Walt's experiences.